ALCOHOLISM

HERMA SILVERSTEIN

ALCOHOLISM

362.29
Sil

19104

Franklin Watts
New York/London/Toronto/Sydney/1990
A Venture Book

Diagrams by Vantage Art

Photographs courtesy of: New York Public Library, Picture Collection: p. 17; Photo Researchers: pp. 21 (Bill Bachman), 25 (Library of Congress), 48 (Christa Armstrong), 49 (Nancy D'Antonio); Culver Pictures: p. 26; C.S.R. Inc.: pp. 38, 104 (Alcoholics Anonymous), 114; Monkmeyer Press Photo: pp. 52 (Mimi Forsyth), 60 top (David Strickler), 87 (Grant LeDuc); World Health Organization: p. 56 (Zafar); Wide World Photos: pp. 60 bottom, 61, 109; Taurus Photos: pp. 69 (Elinor Beckwith), 97 (Laimute Druskis); Woodfin Camp and Associates: p. 78 (Leif Skoogfors); Picture Group: p. 112 (Michael Grecco).

Library of Congress Cataloging-in-Publication Data

Silverstein, Herma.
Alcoholism / Herma Silverstein.
p.   cm.—(A Venture book)
Summary: Discusses how alcohol affects the body and the lives of
both alcoholics and those closest to them.
Includes bibliographical references and index.
ISBN 0-531-10879-1
1. Alcoholism—Juvenile literature.   2. Alcoholics—
Rehabilitation—United States—Juvenile literature.
[1. Alcoholism.]   I. Title.   II. Series.
HV5066.S55   1990
362.29'2—dc20
90-12578   CIP   AC

To Ben
with my love,
one day at a time

CONTENTS

ALCOHOLISM

PROLOGUE

Ted staggered across the street. The monster with the yellow claws and bloody face was chasing him again. *Can't let it get me.* He gulped a swig of bourbon. *There. Liquid monster zapper.*

Got to get home. Get some sleep. Folks'll have a stroke if I cut school again. Probably flunk anyway. And it'll be old Mr. Wiley's fault. Giving those tough chemistry exams. What does he think, we're in college? If I'd had Miss Thornton for chemistry, she'd a given me at least a C.

Ted weaved down the sidewalk. *Got to get to bed. Told Miss T I'd hang posters for the senior prom. It **was** tomorrow, wasn't it? Why can't I remember?*

All Susan's fault. Telling me she wouldn't go to the prom with me if I didn't quit drinking. And after I blew my whole allowance on her corsage. Well, who cares if she breaks our date? Susan's always picking on me lately. Just like my folks. Saying I drink too *much. Saying I should go to AA. That I'm an . . . I am **not** an alcoholic. Alcoholics are bums who sleep in doorways. Bums go to AA. Just because I like to get smashed once in a while doesn't make me a drunk.*

Ted felt the monster's foul breath on his neck. He tried to run, but his feet moved as if he were shackled. He stumbled into a doorway in front of a building. The monster disappeared. *Can't fool me. You're hiding in the alley until I come out. Well, I'll just stay here until morning. I know you're scared of daylight.*

"Te-ed. We're going to get you, Ted."

Those voices again. Where did they come from?

"Don't try to run, Ted. You can't escape us." The voices laughed with a grating rasp, like corpses from the grave.

"Leave me alone!" Ted peeked around the doorway. Everything was a blur. *Only one way to get rid of those voices.*

He took another swallow of bourbon. The liquid seared his stomach and squeezed his insides. He threw up. Blood swam in the vomit.

"Te-ed," the voices chorused. "Look!"

A yellow claw crept around the doorway. It turned into a black snake. Ted screamed and screamed as the snake slithered close to his throat.

Quickly Ted guzzled the rest of his bourbon. But the snake didn't go away. *Whas wrong with thish stuff? That creep at the liquor store musta sold me rotgut.* He threw the bottle at the snake. Glass shattered on the sidewalk. *Have to get another bottle. One more drink'll blow that snake to smithereens.*

(12)

Ted stumbled from the building. His foot slipped in his vomit and he fell. He crawled out of the doorway, through the vomit and broken glass. The snake slithered after him. Ted tried to get up, but he couldn't. The snake gained on him. The voices laughed louder. Ted crawled faster, wincing as glass shards bore into his knees.

Got to get home. Where was home? He fought to remember. But his mind was as black as the night. *Phone someone to come get me. I'll call . . . who? Used to have lots of friends. Can't remember their names. Call the folks. No. Can't do that. Promised them I'd stay off the booze.*

Ted's stomach squeezed. There was something different about the pain this time. Like a thousand knives stabbing his gut. Maybe that doctor his folks dragged him to was right, and his liver was bummed out. Nah. It was just the voices making his stomach hurt.

"Te-ed," the voices chanted. "We have you now. You're ours forever."

Ted's heart felt as if he were pumping iron. *Tired. I'm so tired.* He shut his eyes. The snake disappeared. The voices hushed. His heart slowed down. And the knives pulled out of his stomach. Nothing to worry about. He'd blacked out hundreds of times. He'd just wake up foggy, not knowing where he was or what he'd done before passing out. Then he'd go home, and everything would be okay.

But everything would not be okay. Because this time was different. This time Ted never woke up.

CHAPTER

1

WHAT IS ALCOHOLISM?

Alcoholism is a fatal disease.

Alcoholism has no cure.

Alcoholism is the number one drug threat in the United States.

Alcoholism is the third cause of early death, behind cancer and heart disease.

Alcoholics *can* recover. *Recover*—but *never* be cured.

While there are many different treatments for alcoholism, the only sure way for alcoholics to stop the disease from destroying their bodies, and thus killing them, is to stop drinking before the disease reaches the fatal stage.

The organization Alcoholics Anonymous (AA) has a saying about alcoholics: "I'm only one drink away from a drunk." As one teenager said, "When I was on booze, my biggest fear was getting through a day without a drink. Now it's that I might pick up that one sucker drink.''

Alcoholism: The Runaway Roller Coaster

The disease of alcoholism has a doubly serious complication. Until the alcoholic stops drinking, the damaging effects of alcohol on the body, such as a diseased liver, cannot be stopped. (Cirrhosis of the liver kills between nine thousand and fourteen thousand alcoholics every year.) Yet with few exceptions, willpower alone is not enough to break addiction to alcohol. In most cases, it is not a sudden determination to stop drinking that makes alcoholics seek help, but rather a series of painful events in their lives caused by their drinking that build to a crisis.

However, in many cases, by the time the crisis occurs, the alcoholic's body has already deteriorated so much that no amount of medical treatment will prevent death. Alcoholism is like a runaway roller coaster. "It ruins everything that matters to you," *New York Times* reporter Nan Robertson, a recovering alcoholic, says in her book *Getting Better: Inside Alcoholics Anonymous.* "In the end, the bottle is your only friend. Alcoholics would rather do anything than stop drinking."

The Myths about Alcoholics

Early in the twentieth century, most people associated the word *alcoholic* with a male bum who drank cheap wine and slept in doorways. There were only a few alcoholic treatment programs, such as the Hazelden Foundation in Minnesota. General hospitals in America did not admit alcoholics for treatment. Instead, alcoholics were considered mentally ill and locked away in the back wards of insane asylums. Therefore, alcoholics had no source for recovery, and most drank themselves to death.

Here were several myths formed about alcoholism:

- only bums became alcoholics

- only men were alcoholics

- alcoholism was a cover-up for a more serious emotional or mental disease

- alcoholics would be so devastated if confronted with their problem that they would become violent

- alcoholics didn't care what damage they caused.

The true facts are that most alcoholics are not bums, but rather high achievers. Several studies have proven that people who lack an overwhelming drive to succeed seem less likely to become addicted to alcohol. As one recovering alcoholic surgeon used to say about himself, "You can't be an alcoholic. You're a surgeon." But telltale signs, such as arranging his operating schedule so he could drink undisturbed, gave him away.

Contrary to old beliefs, there have always been women alcoholics. But they were merely diagnosed

During the nineteenth century, alcoholics were generally regarded as mentally ill patients and were committed to insane asylums.

as suffering from depression or anxiety rather than alcoholism. In fact, women make up one-third of AA's membership today.

As to alcoholics not caring what hurt and damage they cause, the truth is that alcoholics usually resent their own behavior. However, because denial is a common symptom of alcoholism (alcoholics won't admit they have a drinking problem), they tend to project their self-hatred onto someone else. For example, an alcoholic who loses his job because he shows up for work drunk every day might say a co-worker was jealous of him and lied about him to get him fired.

Alcohol: The Gateway to
Crime and Drug Abuse

The organization that calculates the most complete statistics on alcoholism in the United States is the National Institution on Alcohol Abuse and Alcoholism (NIAAA), in Washington, D.C. In 1986, the NIAAA reported that eighteen million American adults and 4.6 million teenagers under age eighteen were alcohol abusers.

According to government studies, excessive use of alcohol in this country claims at least 100,000 lives each year, twenty-five times as many as all illegal drugs combined. In 1986, there were 1,793,300 drunk driving arrests in the United States; drunk drivers caused approximately 23,000 traffic deaths; about 174,000 state prison inmates drank heavily before committing crimes of rape, burglary, and assault; alcohol abuse was associated with 70 percent of the 4,000 drowning deaths, and 30 percent of the 30,000 suicides. At least 45 percent of the nation's 250,000 homeless are alcoholics.

In addition, alcoholism accounts for more family problems than any other single cause. In 1987, one in four families reported a problem with liquor at home. Alcoholism accounts for between 25 percent and 50 percent of the violence committed between husbands and wives, and for one-third of child-molestation cases.

The number one killer of fifteen to twenty-four-year-olds is drunk driving accidents. Two out of every five children have tasted wine coolers before age thirteen. In 1987, a *My Weekly Reader* study reported that 41 percent of fifth-graders were pressured by peers to drink. Nearly five million adolescents, or three in ten, have drinking problems. Most kids who have drinking problems also abuse other drugs. Experts see this trend of multiple drug abuse among adults as well. "Even a coke head has to sleep," says Michael Ford, president of the National Association of Addiction Treatment Programs. "When he does, he turns to alcohol . . . and alcoholics resort to drugs to treat hangovers." As the director of one addiction treatment center said, "That's like switching seats on the *Titanic.*"

Children and Alcohol Abuse

Kids are starting to drink heavily at earlier ages today. Kent, now age twenty-two, began drinking at age ten, was hooked on alcohol at eleven, and by age

(19)

twelve started every morning with a glass of tequila. When he was fourteen, he drank one beer at a rock concert and blacked out. "I woke up feeling like a .22 bullet was ricocheting around inside me," he recalled. That's when he got help.

The younger a child starts drinking the greater the risk of becoming dependent on alcohol, as children's nervous systems are not yet fully developed, and alcohol is absorbed into their bodies faster, making them more susceptible than adults to alcohol poisoning. Young people get more drunk on less alcohol and stay drunk longer. In addition, alcohol stunts young people's emotional growth and prevents them from developing the judgment and coping skills they need as adults.

Many experts agree that the main reason children and teenagers are becoming alcoholics is low self-esteem. Sometimes these children have been neglected or abused by their parents, making them feel unwanted. Or they have been pressured by parents to achieve, and if they fail they feel worthless.

A History of Alcoholism

In 1966 the American Medical Association (AMA) declared that alcoholism was a disease, not the result of a person's low morale. The AMA defined alcoholism as "an illness characterized by preoccupation with alcohol and loss of control over its consumption such as to lead usually to intoxication. . . ." The National Council on Alcoholism elaborated upon this definition

*Today younger children, some barely into
their teens, are beginning to drink heavily.*

by saying alcoholism is a "chronic, progressive, and potentially fatal disease marked by repeated drinking that causes trouble in the drinker's personal, professional or family life. . . ."

The manual of psychiatric disorders published by the American Psychiatric Association describes three patterns of alcohol abuse:

- regular daily drinking of large amounts

- regular heavy drinking limited to weekends

- long periods of sobriety punctuated by heavy drinking binges lasting for weeks or months.

The idea of alcoholism as a disease did not begin with the AMA's declaration. The earliest known alcohol consumption dates back to 4000 B.C. Clay tablets have been found written by the Mesopotamians that record amounts of alcohol drunk by Mesopotamians and list recipes for using alcohol as a solvent in medicines. Part of the code of Hammurabi of Babylonia, written in 1700 B.C., limits the sale and drinking of alcohol. In ancient China drunkards were executed.

Euripides, an ancient Greek tragedy writer, was the first person to describe a drunken blackout. In his play *The Bacchae,* the mother of Pentheus, king of Thebes, tears her son to pieces in a drunken frenzy, mistaking him for a lion. She presents his head to Cadmus, her father, before she realizes her mistake.

The first recorded temperance movements (organizations whose purpose is to discourage people from drinking), were formed in ancient China and Egypt.

The single most important temperance document in history is the Bible, which contains more than 150 references to alcohol. The book of Proverbs, for example, says, "Wine is a mocker, strong drink is raging: and whosoever is deceived thereby is not wise." In 1673 the Puritan preacher Increase Mather wrote "Drink is in itself a good creature of God . . . but the abuse of drink is from Satan. . . ."

The word *alcoholism* was coined in 1849 by a Swedish physician, Magnus Huss, in his volumes entitled, *Chronic Alcoholism*. But the first American to define alcoholism as a disease was Dr. Benjamin Rush of Philadelphia, the most respected physician of his time, and a signer of the Declaration of Independence. In his 1784 tract entitled, "Effects of Ardent Spirits on the Human Mind and Body," Dr. Rush concluded that alcohol was an addictive drug, and described "habitual drunkenness" as involuntary. Rush attached a list to his tract called, "A Moral and Physical Thermometer," that resembles modern descriptions of alcoholism's progress from general drunkenness to the degeneration of bodily organs, causing death.

From the 1800s through the 1830s, alcohol consumption in the United States reached 7.10 gallons per person per year, the heaviest drinking era in American history. By the 1840s, perhaps as a result of Dr. Rush's tract, temperance movements such as the Women's Christian Temperance Union swept the United States, and alcohol consumption fell to 3.10 gallons per person per year.

In 1840, the Washingtonians, a forerunner of Alcoholics Anonymous, was established in Baltimore, Maryland. The organization consisted of a group of recovered alcoholics who helped other alcoholics learn how to avoid the temptation to drink again. Abraham Lincoln said of the Washingtonians, "Those whom they desire to convince and persuade are . . . not demons, nor even the worst of men."

The temperance movement reached its peak with the passage of Prohibition, the Eighteenth Amendment to the Constitution, in January 1920, which outlawed the commercial manufacture and distribution of alcohol. Prohibition's focus on ridding the nation of alcohol altogether temporarily ended the public's belief that alcoholism was a disease. Although there was a 35 percent to 50 percent drop in alcohol consumption during Prohibition, the law resulted in outraged reactions from citizens across the country, becoming the most controversial of all amendments to the Constitution, and the only one ever repealed. When Prohibiton was ended in 1933, the concept that alcoholism is a disease was reborn.

Is Alcoholism a Disease?

In 1935, E. M. Jellinek, a physiologist who later founded the Yale School of Alcohol Studies, headed a research group on alcoholism that concluded that treating alcoholics was useless without treating alcoholism itself as a disease. His book *Phases in the Drinking History of Alcoholics,* published in 1946, declared that alcoholism follows a predictable pattern, from social drinking to secret drinking to blackouts.

Many women organized temperance movements throughout the United States, often attacking drinking establishments, as depicted in this pen-and-ink drawing published in 1874.

*This picture, taken during Prohibition, shows
government agents destroying 749 cases of beer.
It was this era that gave rise to
the bootlegging of liquor.*

Jellinek differed from Dr. Rush in that instead of seeing alcoholism as a disease caused by alcohol alone, Jellinek claimed the disease was caused by the interaction between alcohol and a person's physical, psychological, and social makeup.

Subsequent research has shown that alcoholism indeed affects the whole person: physically, mentally, and spiritually. Professionals say it is only by treating all three aspects of a person that alcoholics can recover. The key word is *recover,* not cure. That is why alcoholics who quit drinking call themselves "recovering."

In 1973 the United States government passed the Federal Rehabilitation Act, which defines alcoholism as a handicap and prohibits federal agencies and federally subsidized institutions from discriminating against the handicapped. For example, public housing cannot be denied alcoholics, nor can businesses discriminate against them in employment.

On the other hand, there are people who disagree with the theory that alcoholism is a disease. One such person is Herbert Fingarette, a professor of philosophy at the University of California in Santa Barbara. Based upon studies of alcohol research papers, he wrote a book titled *Heavy Drinking: The Myth of Alcoholism as a Disease,* in which he claims that nobody has found a biological cause for alcoholism; there is no evidence of a genetic factor that leaves alcoholics unable to control their behavior; and there is no medical treatment that has been shown to be effective. Fingarette claims recovery rates for those in rehabilitation programs are about the same as for those not in such programs who are left to stop drinking on their own. Moreover, he claims that some alcoholics can even learn to drink moderately.

In addition, says Fingarette, there are certain times when alcoholics are more likely to get better, regardless of treatment. For example, highly motivated, economically well-off alcoholics "go into treatment when they are desperate to change. This is exactly the time when, treatment program or not, alcoholics are most likely to improve."

One problem in defining alcoholism as a disease is defining who exactly is an alcoholic. Where does heavy drinking end and alcohol abuse begin? The answers to these questions seem to vary from decade to decade. Between 1950 and 1960, movies and books portrayed heroes having several martinis at business lunches and getting drunk at parties. Now such drinking is considered excessive. Enoch Gordis, director of the National Institute on Alcohol Abuse and Alcoholism, says alcoholics continue to drink despite the consequences, even when alcohol overwhelms their intelligence and judgments.

While the debate rages over whether or not alcoholism is a disease, eighteen million Americans are drinking themselves to death. Whatever alcoholism is, there is one unquestionable fact: the only surefire cure for alcoholism is never to drink. Ever again.

Dr. Lyman Boynton, the surgeon who thought he couldn't be an alcoholic because he was a surgeon, has been "on the wagon" since 1982. He believes much can be done to find the causes of alcoholism and then to give individual treatment to alcoholics based upon these causes. Today Dr. Boynton heads a substance-abuse program at San Francisco's Kaiser Permanente Hospital. "Now," he says, "I have all the things in recovery that I was looking for in a bottle."

CHAPTER

2

THE CAUSES OF ALCOHOLISM AND ITS EFFECTS ON THE BODY

Alcoholism is often called the disease of denial. Denial means refusing to admit the truth about a situation. That is why alcoholism is difficult for doctors to diagnose. If a patient does not admit to having a drinking problem, the symptoms he or she complains of can be attributed to other diseases which have the same symptoms. For example, alcoholics can blame feelings of nausea on the flu or headaches, or memory loss on old age.

In 1987 the American Psychiatric Association listed three criteria for doctors to diagnose alcoholism:

- physiological problems, such as hand tremors and blackouts;

- psychological problems, such as an obsessive desire to drink;

- behavioral problems that disrupt social or work life.

Can Alcoholism Be Inherited?

As research on the causes of alcoholism continues, studies of twins have greatly aided scientists in proving a genetic cause for alcoholism. Identical twins share 100 percent of their inherited genes. Fraternal twins share only 50 percent. Therefore, it should follow that if alcoholism is inherited, identical twins of an alcoholic parent should be twice as likely to become alcoholics as fraternal twins. Studies have proved this theory is true: the risk for becoming an alcoholic is 60 percent higher for identical twins of alcoholics born to an alcoholic parent, and only 30 percent more likely for fraternal twins born to an alcoholic parent.

Studies of adopted children have also provided proof of a genetic factor in alcoholism. In the 1970s, Dr. Donald Goodwin, head of the Department of Psychiatry at the University of Kansas School of Medicine, studied 133 Danish men adopted as children by nonalcoholic parents. He divided the men into two groups: those with an alcoholic biological parent and those with nonalcoholic biological parents. His results showed that the sons of an alcoholic parent had drinking problems four times as often as the sons of nonalcoholic parents, and that daughters of alcoholic mothers were three times as likely to become alcoholics.

Dr. Goodwin's research does not mean that all children of alcoholics (COAs) will become alcoholics. Statistics show that 30 percent of alcoholics have no family history of alcoholism. However, his results also mean that COAs can be warned that drinking like their peers do could lead to alcoholism.

Another study on the causes of alcoholism was performed by Dr. C. Robert Cloninger, a professor of psychiatry at Washington University in St. Louis, Missouri. He conducted his research in Sweden, where adoption records are available for scientific research. He studied 1,775 adopted men and women, more than a third of whom had an alcoholic biological parent. As Dr. Cloninger reviewed the work and police records of his subjects, two distinct types of alcoholics emerged, giving evidence that alcoholism may have more than one form.

Dr. Cloninger called the first group (about 25 percent of the total) made up mostly of men, Type 1 alcoholics. Type I subjects had started drinking heavily in adolescence, had bad work and police records, and showed little success after treatment programs. Type I personalities are highly anxious, emotionally dependent upon others, and shy. Sons of Type I alcoholics were nine times as likely to become alcoholics as children of nonalcoholics.

The second group of alcoholics, called Type 2, included both men and women, and made up about 75 percent of the study's alcoholics. Type 2 alcoholics started chronic drinking after age twenty-five, rarely had trouble with the law, and often successfully stopped drinking. Dr. Cloninger found Type 2's to be impulsive, distractible, and emotionally detached. Children of Type 2 alcoholics were twice as likely to have drinking problems as children of nonalcoholics.

Dr. Cloninger also found four environmental influences for alcoholism in Type 2 alcoholics: being reared by the biological mother for more than six months, being older at the time of adoption, spending more time in the hospital prior to adoption, and having a father with a lower occupational status.

Dr. Cloninger's findings have given scientists a road map to link genes with specific behavior patterns in alcoholics. "What we learned from the adoption studies," he said, "is not that nature was important or nurture was important, but that both are important."

To determine what genetic characteristics children of alcoholics inherit, and how genetics and environment combine to cause a person to become an alcoholic, researchers have begun to study adoptive families over a long period of time to discover environmental influences on each sibling in an adopted child's family.

Researchers are also hoping to develop medical tests to identify biochemical reactions in the body, such as a particular brain wave pattern, that appear only in children with a family history of alcohol abuse. Then they can help identify COAs who are at the highest risk of becoming alcoholics and warn these people about alcohol's possible effects on their bodies.

One researcher who did find a biochemical marker is Dr. Henri Begleiter, of the State University of New York Health Science Center in Brooklyn. Studying children between seven and fourteen years old, he found that sons of alcoholics display the same abnormal brain waves as adult alcoholics who have been sober at least five years. In addition, he found that electrical brain waves of children of alcoholics look

(33)

and react differently from brain waves of children of nonalcoholics. And yet these children had never had a drop of alcohol.

Dr. Marc Shuckit, a psychiatrist at the San Diego Veterans Administration Medical Center at La Jolla, California, matched individual sons of alcoholics of ages eighteen to twenty-five, who were not alcoholics themselves, each with another man of the same age, similar religion, race, education, drinking history, height, and weight, but who had no family history of alcoholism. Each pair was fed pure alcohol on several occasions. While the pairs showed identical alcohol blood-levels, there were four main differences: the sons of alcoholics did not feel as drunk as sons from non-alcoholic families; swayed and slurred their words less; had better hand-eye coordination; and did not experience as intense hormonal changes. Other studies have shown the same to be true for young adult daughters of male alcoholics. COA's higher tolerance for alcohol may make them likely to drink larger doses of alcohol to achieve the same effect, paving the way for excessive drinking.

Findings such as Dr. Shuckit's may provide clues in the search for specific genes involved in alcoholism. If a particular gene that causes alcoholism is identified, then scientists may be able to manufacture a gene that prevents a person from becoming an alcoholic. The alcoholic-preventing gene could be transplanted onto the appropriate chromosome and replace the defective alcoholic-causing gene.

What spurs scientists on to discover an alcoholism gene is the fact that some people apparently inherit severe reactions to alcohol. For example, an enzyme deficiency in some Asians causes facial flushing, queasiness, and other unpleasant reactions after drinking small amounts of alcohol. These reactions discourage many Asians from drinking. In fact, studies have shown that Asians have a lower rate of alcoholism than do other ethnic groups.

On the other hand, some ethnic groups tend to become alcoholics more frequently. "Alcoholism is like wildfire," says National Black Alcoholism Council chairman Maxine Womble, but "in the black community the fire tends to spread much, much faster and burn a whole lot longer." Likewise, alcoholism is a common problem for American Indians and people of Irish descent.

Physiological Effects
of Alcohol

What are the effects of alcohol on the body?

Alcohol, even small amounts, affects every organ in the body the minute a person takes one drink. The more a person drinks, the more damage is done to the body. Alcohol changes brain cells, causing impaired physical coordination, memory loss, dulled senses, and brain damage. A chronic condition called Wenicke's disease is common, in which eye movement is paralyzed, and rapid mental deterioration occurs.

Alcohol stimulates the stomach to secrete gastric acid, which inflames the stomach lining, causing painful peptic ulcers. Alcohol eats up the stomach and intestines, causing bleeding and stomach cancer. In the heart, deterioration of the heart muscle occurs, resulting in strokes, high blood pressure, and heart attacks.

Similar to the destruction of the immune system in AIDS, alcohol abuse prevents white blood cells from fighting infection, increasing the risk of viral or bacterial infections. Alcohol also prevents the manufacture of red blood cells, causing anemia. Studies are now underway to discover if heavy drinking causes AIDS to appear more quickly in infected carriers.

Because specific enzymes called "Cytochrome P-450's" turn certain chemicals in the body into carcinogens when combined with alcohol, heavy drinking has been linked to cancer of the liver, lungs, pancreas, colon, rectum, and breasts. Even women who drink moderately (three to nine drinks a week) have a 30 percent to 50 percent greater chance over nondrinkers of developing breast cancer.

In the reproductive system, high doses of alcohol reduce the number of sex hormones. In men, this means a lower sex drive, shrunken testicles, impotence, and enlarged breasts. For women, lower sex hormones cause irregular menstrual cycles and their ovaries to stop functioning, resulting in sterility.

Fetal Alcohol Syndrome

Pregnant women who drink even small amounts may give birth to babies with Fetal Alcohol Syndrome (FAS), resulting in severe birth defects, including mental retardation. This is because some of whatever a pregnant woman eats or drinks passes through the placenta into the body of the fetus to provide nourishment for the baby. Therefore, if a pregnant mother gets drunk, so does her unborn child. The same is true of women who drink while they breast-feed. Alcohol passes into the baby's body through the breast milk, in effect getting the baby drunk along with the mother. According to the *Los Angeles Times,* an estimated fifty thousand FAS babies are born each year in the United States.

Like infants born to drug addicts, babies born to alcoholic women can experience painful withdrawal symptoms of alcoholism, such as delirium tremens (d.t.'s), as soon as the umbilical cord is cut. Symptoms of delirium tremens, which can be fatal, include violent trembling, hallucinations, and confusion.

In his book *The Broken Cord,* author Michael Doris, who unknowingly adopted an FAS baby, describes what it was like raising his child Adam (not his real name). In some cases, he says, FAS babies "enter the world tainted with stale wine. Their amniotic fluid literally reeks of Thunderbird or Ripple, and the whole operating theater stinks like the scene of a three-day party. Nurses close their eyes at the memory."

Other symptoms of FAS include premature birth, a small head, flat nasal bridges, and shortened eyelids. FAS babies are commonly hyperactive, fail to grow at the rate of other children their age, and have short attention spans, learning disabilities, and memory problems. They often lack basic judgment skills or the ability to predict the consequences of their be-

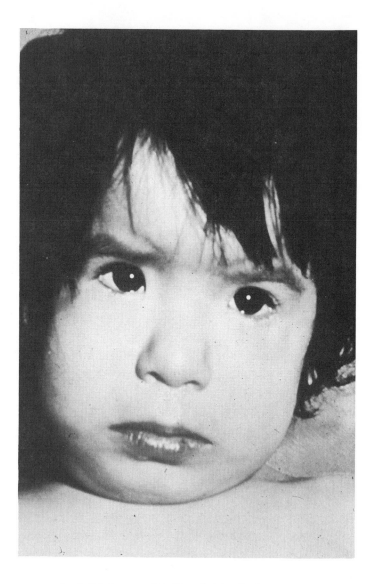

*A child born with Fetal Alcohol Syndrome
may have such birth defects as
a flat midface, a low nasal bridge,
and a short nose.*

havior. Many FAS babies become adults who are unable to take care of themselves without help. For example, Adam lives in a group house and sees his parents once a week. His father says, ". . . in our heart of hearts, we still expect that there's going to be this key turned in Adam's brain that opens the door to what's in the world, or who he is, or who we are . . . but intellectually I know that's not going to happen. . . . His mother drank when she was pregnant, and the damage was done.''

Liver Damage

Of all the body organs affected by alcohol, the liver suffers the most. The liver's job is to process nutrients in food to other parts of the body, and filter poisons from the blood, and break them down to be excreted. Alcohol is high in calories (there are 110 calories per jigger of 90-proof liquor), and the liver processes the alcohol instead of nutrients, sometimes leading to malnutrition. The high calories in alcohol cause fat to accumulate in the liver, an early symptom of alcoholic liver disease.

Next occurs scarring of the liver tissue; this stops the liver from filtering poisons from the blood. The liver cells die, resulting in cirrhosis, or total degeneration of the liver, which is fatal. About one-half of those who develop cirrhosis will die within five years. A recent study suggests that men who take three drinks a day and women who take only one and a half drinks a day may be at increased risk of developing cirrhosis of the liver.

Alcohol overdose is a major cause of death among alcoholics. Often the overdose is caused by mixing drugs such as cocaine or heroin with alcohol. Other times the overdose is caused by mixing alcohol with drugs a doctor has prescribed to regulate an illness. In some cases, even one drink can be fatal, because the liver cannot effectively filter both the alcohol and the drug. Therefore, both remain in the body and accumulate to poisonous levels.

In addition, when an alcoholic's liver has learned to work faster than normal to clear the body of excess alcohol, the liver also removes the prescription drug from the body faster than normal, preventing the drug from having enough time to do its job before it is excreted.

The only difference between alcohol and drug abuse is that alcohol is legal, making drinking acceptable. Thus, "tying one on" at a Super Bowl or New Years' Eve party seems harmless enough, and the person is not regarded with the same contempt as an addict shooting up with heroin. Yet the effects of drug and alcohol abuse on the body are equally devastating, and the final effect is identical: death.

Susan's Story

Today alcohol treatment centers are admitting more young people as patients. Eighteen-year-old Susan is similar to many young alcoholics:

"I took my first drink when I was ten. My dad went around smashed every night. 'I had a rotten day at work,' he'd say. 'I need a drink.' If alcohol worked for him, maybe it would for me, too. I had rotten days at school because I was twenty pounds heavier than anyone in my class. I never got invited to parties. I'd go on crazy diets, lose weight, then gain it all back the minute I ate normal again. I'd tried the binge-and-purge routine, but I couldn't stand throwing up.

"That first drink did the trick. I felt great, even pretty. So when other girls in fifth grade were at a slumber party, I had a party with booze. I'd sneak a bottle up to my room. My folks never even missed it. I lost weight, too. At twelve, when I bottomed out and went to a rehab center, I learned that I'd been starving myself to death. You can get high faster on an empty stomach, and the buzz lasts longer. Who wanted to kill the good feeling with food? The weird-est thing is my parents kept saying how proud of me they were that I'd started caring about my weight. All I cared about was hearing that three-o'clock bell ring so I could have a drink.

"Then the bad stuff started. My hands shook all day, and I couldn't concentrate on what the teacher said. I'd forget homework assignments. Then one day this girl yelled at me for not even saying I was sorry I'd torn up all her valentines. I thought she was crazy. Why would I do something awful like that? Then the teacher asked if I'd brought the girl new valentines for the ones I'd torn up. If the teacher said that, then I must have done what the girl said. How come I didn't remember?

"During the next few months I'd get in trouble for doing things I couldn't remember doing. I thought maybe I had a multiple personality like that girl in the movie *Sybil*. I started having killer headaches, and my stomach felt as if a bonfire were blazing inside. One day my class was playing kickball at recess, and I fainted. My folks took me to a doctor. She asked me how much I drank. How'd she know?

"Then she said something that really scared me. She said a part of my brain was dying every time I drank. That's why I had blackouts, which meant forgetting what I'd done or where I'd been for a minute, an hour, or even a whole day. The doctor said if I didn't stop drinking, I might do something criminal that I wouldn't remember.

"What she said scared me so much that I told my folks I'd go to a rehab place. I figured if all those famous people could stand it, so could I. The first few days were the pits. My body was withdrawing from the alcohol, which makes you sicker than a dog. I didn't know twelve-year-olds could have the d.t.'s. I thought only winos had hallucinations and the shakes and puked all over the place.

"There were a bunch of other kids there, and we met with a counselor every day in group therapy. We talked about why we started drinking and how we could stay sober. I went to my fist AA meeting while I was there. That was another thing I was wrong about. I thought AA was for the same bums who had the d.t.'s. But there's all sorts of people in AA, from winos to high-class executives to famous movie stars. AA has a program called "The Twelve Steps." If you do the steps, it's a lot easier to stay sober.

"I also found out that a lot of kids started drinking for the same reason as me—because they were fat or had acne or just thought they were ugly and stupid. And some drank for even more horrible reasons, like getting beaten up, or worse, by their folks.

"Because I overdid the alcohol bit, I'll never be able to drink like normal people. Actually, the bottom line is I'll never be able to drink at all—ever again. Not if I want to stay alive."

Loren Archer, the deputy director of the National Institute on Alcohol Abuse and Alcoholism, describes the difference between alcoholics and heavy drinkers as the "cucumber into-pickle" theory. "The alcoholics are . . . pickles, addicted to drink and showing symptoms of total dependence . . . alcohol abusers are cucumbers turning into pickles. And once you're a pickle, there's no way you can go back to being a cucumber again."

CHAPTER

3

FROM SOCIAL DRINKER TO DRUNK: THE FOUR STAGES TO BECOMING AN ALCOHOLIC

"First the man takes a drink,
and then the drink takes a drink,
and finally the drink takes the man."
—Old Chinese proverb

Addiction to alcohol is a gradual process in which a person passes through four general stages, the final one being the fatal stage. Each of these stages is characterized by increased physical and mental deterioration. Just as people do not become drug addicts by smoking one marijuana cigarette, or develop eating disorders by binging and purging one time on chocolate cake, so alcoholics usually do not show severe symptoms of alcoholism when they first start to drink.

Addiction develops when a person habitually craves immediate gratification from a substance such as alcohol; the gratification is followed by delayed, harmful effects; and the person continues the harmful behavior in spite of the harmful effects, because the addict is unable to control his or her behavior. For example, one drink may make a person feel good. But too many drinks makes a person drunk and ends in a hangover. The hangover leads to a craving for alcohol's "good" effects again. Thus a cycle of alcohol abuse begins.

Although the gradual process of addiction makes it difficult to tell a heavy drinker from an alcoholic, there are some clues: heavy drinkers like to drink for the "good" feelings that go with alcohol. They continue to drink heavily until the discomforts outweigh the pleasures. Then either they quit drinking altogether or cut back to "normal" social drinking. Neither choice requires great willpower.

Alcoholics, on the other hand, *cannot stop drinking,* no matter how much the harmful effects of alcohol outweigh the pleasures. They drink even when they know that to do so will get them in trouble—before a boss's dinner party, giving an important speech, or taking a final exam. Gradually alcohol becomes the prime requirement for having a good time, whether the person is going to a football game, a movie, or out to dinner.

Job stress, marital problems, even small upsets such as a flat tire or the television going on the blink, are considered reasons to go on a binge. For young people the reason could be a broken date, flunking a test, or an argument with a parent. The amount of alcohol consumed increases as the alcoholic's tolerance for alcohol grows, and it takes more drinks to "feel good." For the alcoholic, liquor has gone from beverage to drug.

The Four Stages

As mentioned, the road to alcoholism can be divided into four stages, or boundaries. The progress from stage one to stage four averages out to fifteen years but can range anywhere from seven to twenty-five years.

Stage One:
In the first stage, a person takes his or her first drink. The effects make him or her feel good. When the effects of alcohol wear off, the drinker returns to normal. There is no physical or emotional pain—the biggest signal of the onset of alcoholism. But the drinker has learned three facts: alcohol is a way to feel better; how much better depends on the amount drunk; and alcohol works every time.

Stage Two:
Now the drinker seeks out regular social drinking in appropriate ways. For example, "the drink before dinner" has been a custom for adults in many American homes for over two centuries. In recent years, the cocktail hour has moved out of the home and into bars, where the custom is now called the "Happy Hour," backing up the drinker's learned experience that drinking is a happy activity.

The social drinker can even get drunk occasionally without experiencing any more serious emotional or physical cost than a hangover the next day, a price he or she is willing to pay for a night on the town. Usually these occasional drinking binges are begun as a celebration of some significant event: a pay raise, a wedding anniversary, or, for teenagers, prom night or high school graduation.

Stage-two drinkers make up rules for drinking, such as "no alcohol before five o'clock." Or a high school student's rule might be, "I'll only drink on weekends." For parents with young children, the rule might be, "I won't drink until the children are asleep for the night."

Stage-two drinkers stick by their rules until the day comes when a businessman looks at his watch and it's only two o'clock. "How will I ever get through three more hours without a martini?" he wonders. The high school student is dying for a drink, but it's only Wednesday. "Thank god it's Friday" has a whole new meaning. The parent with young children is itching to fix that first drink of the day, but the children's bedtime isn't for another hour.

In stage two, drinking, even getting drunk, is still a safe experience, like swinging on a rope over a creek and back again without falling into the water. As drinkers move into stage three, however, they not only fall into the water, but get caught in a powerful undertow as well.

Stage Three:
By stage three, drinkers have crossed the boundary from social drinker to alcoholic. The crossover is signaled by a change in the drinker's attitude from *anticipation* of drinking to *preoccupation* with drinking.

*Alcoholism may begin with social drinking.
Here, a group of teenagers drink soda and
beer at a get-together.*

*During "happy hour," a young professional downs
two mugs of beer as his friends cheer him on.*

The person's whole day revolves around drinking, and he or she will go to any lengths to change his or her lifestyle to drink. For example, a person who used to enjoy surfing will stop the sport because to surf he must be sober, and that interferes with his drinking.

Those self-imposed drinking rules invented in stage two are redesigned to indulge the increased craving for alcohol. The businessperson says, "So it's not five o'clock yet. But it's my day off, and I deserve to relax. I'll just have one drink while I read the paper." The high school student says, "So it's not the weekend yet. But finals ended today. Everyone gets smashed after finals." The parent of young children says, "So it's not their bedtime yet. But those kids are driving me crazy. I'll have a drink to calm down."

Finally the rules for when they will *not* drink change to a rigid schedule of when they *will* drink. The businessperson plans meetings for lunch, where "We can have a drink and discuss business without interruptions." In contrast to social drinkers, alcoholics get extremely upset if an unexpected event interrupts their scheduled drinking time.

For instance, an alcoholic's friends suggest eating at a certain restaurant. The alcoholic knows that particular restaurant does not serve alcohol. She says, "Oh, that place has terrible service," then suggests another restaurant where she knows alcohol is served. Or the parent who only drinks after the kids are asleep comes home to find one of the children has the flu. In stage two, that parent would have willingly given up his/her nightly drink to take care of the child. Now, however, that parent's response might be, "Why did he have to get sick tonight?" Or, "Isn't there some medicine he can take so he'll go to sleep?"

The high school student comes home Friday afternoon, relieved drinking time is finally here, only to learn the family is going to visit Grandmother for the weekend. In stage two, the student would have been disappointed at giving up his weekend drinking, but would have accepted the change in plans without much fuss. Now, however, his response is, "I already have plans." Or, "We went to Grandmother's for Thanksgiving. Why are we going again now?"

During stage three, the family usually realizes one of its members has a drinking problem and tries to talk the person into getting help. The alcoholic usually denies there is a problem, or swears never to have another drink. Then the alcoholic starts to hide liquor all over the house in order to sneak drinks. Amazingly, alcoholics tend to stash their liquor in the same places. The laundry hamper, inside a heating vent, or under the mattress are common examples.

Certain habits typical of alcoholism develop. When a couple give a party, the husband or wife alcoholic will have a couple of drinks in the kitchen or behind the bar while making the guests' drinks. Or, knowing they are going to someone's house for dinner where liquor will not be served, alcoholics gulp down a few drinks beforehand to "tide them over."

Another indicator that social drinkers have become alcoholics is the high emotional price they now pay for every drink. They are totally dependent upon alcohol to get through the day, yet drinking no longer

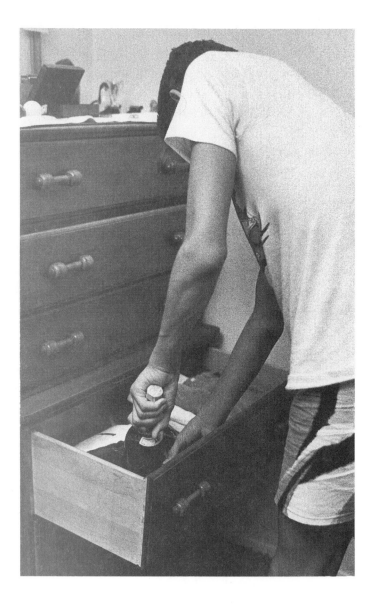

*Stashing liquor bottles in secret
places usually indicates the advanced
stage of a drinking problem.*

makes them feel good. Therefore, they subconsciously invent excuses as to why they drink and why a particular drinking binge made them feel bad. These defenses are called rationalizations. For example, the teenage alcoholic might say, "Who wouldn't need a drink after such a hard math final?" Another alcoholic might rationalize a particularly bad drinking experience by saying, "I got drunk because I drank on an empty stomach."

While such defensive rationalizations make alcoholics feel better about their drinking, the excuses also cause alcoholics to deny their emotions. As the disease progresses, alcoholics lose all sense of emotion. Most people rationalize when they fail at something. But when confronted with the reality of the situation, nonalcoholics see the reality and accept responsibility for their mistakes.

As alcoholics' drinking binges become more painful, their ability to rationalize bizarre behavior caused by their drinking becomes so embedded in their personalities that they lose touch with reality altogether. For instance, when an alcoholic says, "I don't have a drinking problem. My problem is migraine headaches," he truly believes this. As alcoholics' destructive behavior worsens, denial of the problem becomes the key to survival. Now, after a painful drinking bout, instead of merely feeling uncomfortable, the alcoholic feels remorse. "That was so dumb to jump in the swimming pool with my clothes on," a woman might say.

This statement soon changes from "that was dumb" to "I'm so dumb." The destructive and bizarre behavior caused by drinking makes alcoholics feel worthless, and soon self-hatred takes over. "I'm so dumb" becomes, "I'm no good." When this happens, stress becomes a chronic condition, and alcoholics feel stressed *even when not drinking*.

Personality changes occur along with the stress. A friendly person becomes hostile, a happy person sad, and a gentle person violent. Drinking to oblivion is now the norm. Suicidal feelings emerge. "I'm so rotten I might as well kill myself," is a typical statement in stage three.

Stage Four:
Nonalcoholics frequently ask, "Why don't these people see what's happening to them and stop drinking?" The answer is, they can't. Alcoholics do *not* know what is happening to themselves. They unload whatever negative feelings they have about their drinking onto others. This is called "projection."

The high school student might say, "My parents are real jerks. All they do is nag." An alcoholic wife says, "My husband never talks to me about my feelings." The alcoholic businessperson says, "My boss is making me crazy. He complains about the least little thing." Whereas in the first stages of alcoholism, people drank to feel good, in stage-four alcoholics are in a chronic state of depression and pain, and therefore drink to feel normal. They frequently "go on the wagon," only to start drinking again in a week, a month, or a day, not knowing why they started drinking again.

In the final stage of alcoholism, three symptoms

appear, which destroy the alcoholic's memory system: blackouts, repression, and euphoric recall. A blackout is a chemically induced period of amnesia. It is not the same as passing out. During a blackout, alcoholics function as if they are aware of what is happening around them. But when they become sober again, they remember nothing about what happened while they were drinking. Thus, if an alcoholic has an argument with someone during a blackout, the other person, unaware that the alcoholic does not know what he is doing, will expect him to apologize later. When the alcoholic acts as if no argument ever occurred, the other person is hurt, while the alcoholic thinks the friend made the incident up.

As the disease progresses, blackouts become more frequent, last longer, and are more unpredictable as to the amount of alcohol necessary to cause them. After a blackout, the alcoholic is haunted by such questions as, "How did I get home last night?" "Where did I leave my car?" "How did I get into this hotel room?"

One alcoholic's blackout involved him taking a round-trip flight to Rome. Upon returning, he told his alcohol counselor he didn't remember buying the ticket or taking the trip. The counselor talked to the man for over an hour, and he made an appointment to return the next day with his wife. Then the man called a taxi and left. A little later, the counselor's secretary told him a cab driver was in the waiting room looking for the man he'd dropped off. The man had asked the cab driver, who still had the man's luggage in his cab, to pick him up in two hours. Only then did the counselor realize that the alcoholic had been discussing his con-

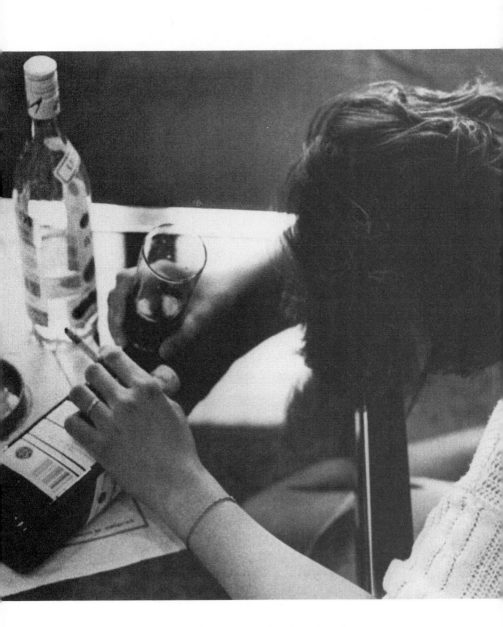

Getting drunk may lead to blackouts,
wherein alcoholics cease to
be aware of what is happening around them.

cern about being in a blackout *while he was in a blackout*. The alcoholic would eventually come out of the blackout, unable to recall either his trip to Italy or his visit to the counselor.

Another man's story is even more tragic. While in a blackout he drove his car into three children riding bicycles and killed one of them. The night before his trial, he committed suicide.

The second symptom that destroys an alcoholic's memory system is repression. From time to time, everyone uses repression as a defense. When an event is too painful to bear, we repress it, or push it back into our subconscious, either to leave it there forever, or to bring it up at a later time when we can emotionally deal with the pain. Alcoholics, on the other hand, use repression constantly. As their behavior produces intense pain and shame day after day, repression of what they do while drunk is their only way to deal with their behavior in order to keep drinking. And alcoholics crave drinking at any cost.

Here is an example of how repression works: A seventeen-year-old girl wakes up late one Saturday morning. Having experienced many blackouts, after which she awoke in a strange bed not knowing how she got there, she is at first relieved to find herself in her own room. But then a flash of memory occurs. Last night she got drunk. She did something horribly embarrassing. She cannot stand the memory, so she blocks it out of her mind. She has breakfast with her family, talking about the great time she had with her boyfriend last night. Then the phone rings, and her boyfriend asks if she has spoken to her parents about whether her car insurance will pay for the accident. "What accident?" the girl asks. The boy says, "You know you totaled my car last night. Right after we had that fight, you took off and rammed my car into the Joneses' fence." The girl, having repressed the accident, truly believes the boy is making up the story so he won't have to tell his parents he wrecked their car. The result of repeated repression is depression and greater loss of reality.

The third alcoholic condition that distorts memory is euphoric recall, the greatest cause of delusions. Euphoric recall describes how alcoholics remember their drinking binges: euphorically, or happily, and with great distortion. For example, at a party, the alcoholic starts telling a story. She weaves around the room and bumps into a valuable vase, knocking it onto the floor. The next day the alcoholic says she told a great story at the party, and everyone thought she was the hit of the evening. The only truthful part of her memory is the telling of the story.

Alcohol depresses the body's brain cells, causing people to be less guarded in their behavior. This is why alcohol seems like an "upper" when actually it is a depressant, or "downer." If people drink excessively over a period of time, eventually they will be incapable of remembering what happened while they were drinking. All they remember is that they felt good.

A tragic example of euphoric recall is the drunk driver. An alcoholic who has been drinking at a party gets ready to leave. A friend offers to drive him home. Highly insulted, the alcoholic either swears he is sober or that he hasn't had that much to drink and is capable of driving himself. He believes he can drive because the effect of the alcohol makes it impossible for him to accurately know he is drunk. He drives home, speeding, weaving from lane to lane, and doesn't see a stoplight. Sailing across the intersection, he crashes head-on with another car, killing the other driver.

In the Los Angeles suburb of Pacific Palisades, four teenagers left a party where they had been drinking heavily. They piled into one of the boys' cars. Going seventy miles an hour, the seventeen-year-old driver lost control of the car and slammed into a tree in the middle of a traffic median. The car exploded into flames. The only way the parents could identify their children was through their dental records.

Drunken Driving

During the past sixteen months ten teenagers who went to Pacific Palisades High School in Los Angeles died in drunk driving accidents. A school psychologist there started the first high school chapter of Alcoholics Anonymous. In keeping with AA's rule of anonymity, students' parents are not informed of their attendance at AA meetings. Other programs started to help teenagers deal with substance abuse were a lunchtime support group for ex-patients of hospital substance abuse treatment, and a mandatory after-school program for students caught using or carrying drugs.

So many children have been killed by drunk drivers that in the 1980's a mother whose child had been killed by a drunk driver formed a national organization called "Mothers Against Drunk Driving"

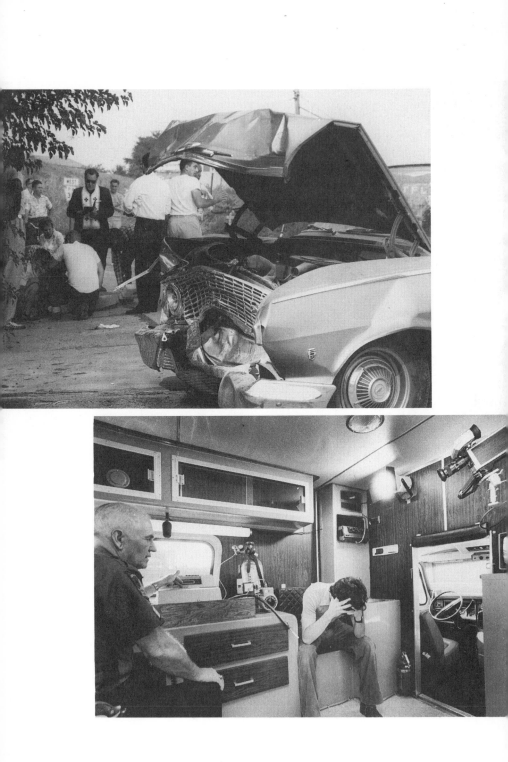

*Facing page (top): A clergyman (left, with book)
performs the last rites for the victims of
a fatal car accident caused by drunk driving.
Facing page (bottom): A police van specially
designed to interview intoxicated drivers is equipped
with a video camera that records the
suspect's response as he is tested for
possible drunk-driving violations.
Above: Members of Mothers Against Drunk
Driving (MADD) hold pictures of loved ones
who died at the hands of drunk drivers*

(MADD). Members of MADD have helped push alcoholism laws through Congress, such as raising the drinking age to twenty-one in all states except Wyoming.

On the road from social drinker to alcoholic, two forces make the alcoholic lose touch with reality: denial and distortion of memory. Eventually it no longer makes sense to ask why alcoholics cannot stop drinking. The truth is they cannot. Yet they are terminally ill with a disease that is a progressive emotional disorder. If not treated, the result for the alcoholic is the same, whether it is intentional or accidental. That result is suicide.

CHAPTER

4

LIVING WITH AN ALCOHOLIC: THE EFFECTS ON THE FAMILY

I didn't cause the alcoholism.
I can't control it.
I can't cure it.
                    —The "Three Cs"
                    of Al-Anon

"Your ole man ain't nothin'!" Dad yelled.

"Shut up," Mom screamed.

It was four A.M. I lay in bed trembling. I was nine years old.

On nights when my father was drinking lots of whiskey, he might sleep for hours; then he'd wake up angry. Someone would become the victim of his rage . . . sometimes it was me. . . . My mother would ask if she could sleep with me, saying, "he's starting to shadow-box in bed, and I don't want a black eye." It made me hate my father when he'd do this to her.

Tonight's fight started at dinner when Dad yelled, "I hate the way you keep the refrigerator," and started pulling food out and throwing it on the floor. My brother leaped on Dad and punched him. I clung to my mother, shaking. Then we cleaned up the mess.

In the morning, none of us would talk about last night. . . . Above all, we knew never to let anyone outside our home know the truth. . . . My sister and I built forts in our room: blankets over crates, blankets hanging from the ceiling. Safe places to crawl into to stay away from Dad. Why wouldn't he stop? we kept asking. If he had been epileptic or mentally retarded, we'd have understood. But none of us understood alcoholism. We didn't know that alcoholism was a disease that affected the whole family.

—Suzanne Somers, actress

Families of alcoholics suffer the same emotional symptoms of the disease as the alcoholic. Studies show that each one of the eighteen million alcoholics in the United States devastates the lives of at least four other people, a total of seventy-two million Americans.

Codependents and Enablers

Physicians have given a name to the illness suffered by these seventy-two million Americans: *codependency*. Codependency is an unconscious addiction to another person's abnormal behavior. The codependent person takes on the alcoholic family member's illness by trying to cure or control the disease. Some family members become so obsessed with stopping the alcoholic's drinking that their entire day revolves around this one goal. As a result, their lives become as disturbed as the alcoholic's. Al-Anon, an organization started in 1951 for families and close friends of alcoholics, has a saying: "The drunk wraps his arms around the bottle. And the family wraps its arms around the drunk."

Codependent people become "enablers." An enabler is a person who unknowingly helps the alcoholic, either by looking the other way and denying the drinking problem exists, or by helping the alcoholic get out of trouble caused by his drinking. For example, an enabler pays the alcoholic's overdue bills; cleans up his vomit; makes excuses to the boss (or the teacher) for the drinker's bizarre behavior (or flunking a test, or failing to turn in homework assignments), hides the liquor, or pours it down the drain.

An enabler lies for the alcoholic. The cover-up allows, or *enables,* the alcoholic to keep drinking. As the alcoholic continually projects his self-hatred onto his family and blames them for his drinking problem, the family starts to believe they really are hateful people and accept the blame for the alcoholic's behavior. A typical accusation is, "If you weren't so demanding (wishy-washy, weak, strong-willed, stubborn, nagging) I'd be just fine." Once families of alcoholics take the blame, they try to correct an imagined fault in themselves that causes the alcoholic to drink. "If only I were a better wife (husband, son, daughter), my husband (wife, father, mother) wouldn't drink." A self-defeating cycle begins.

The wife fixes dinner late or early, depending

upon her husband's drinking routine. Parents pretend it is just an adolescent desire for privacy when their children shut themselves in their rooms and lock their doors immediately after school. Even when children's rooms smell like a brewery, parents will find another reason besides alcohol for the odor. The husband makes excuses why his wife can't attend business dinners, answer the phone, or drive a carpool. The entire family pampers, nags, begs, or yells at the alcoholic to stop drinking.

Of all the codependents, children are hit the hardest. They suffer such childhood traumas as witnessing violence, sexual abuse, and drunken accidents. These children cannot talk about their emotions of terror, anger, and grief, because of the alcoholic family's unspoken, but strictly enforced, rule of silence about what goes on in the home. They continually have to make excuses why they can't invite their friends over, why their parents can't make it to "parent's night" at school, or, in situations where the alcoholic parent is violent, how they got that bruise, cut, or bump on their face.

Often these children unconsciously act out their feelings of anger at and abandonment by the alcoholic parent by negative behavior, such as shoplifting or taking drugs. They will settle for any attention, even punishment, in order to get the alcoholic parent to notice *them* instead of the bottle.

Whatever method the family tries to get the alcoholic to stop drinking fails. As their failures mount, their feelings of worthlessness grow. So do their defenses. Like alcoholics, they start using rationalization as a defense against the alcoholic's abusive behavior. And like alcoholics, they project their negative feelings onto others, and eventually lose their ability to feel emotions.

Support Groups For
Families of Alcoholics

Families of alcoholics need treatment just as much as alcoholics. Yet, like the alcoholic, they usually wait until they hit rock bottom before seeking help. Author Nan Robertson advises family members: "Don't protect [the alcoholic]. Don't call the boss to say, 'Fred is sick today and can't come to the office.' Don't pour the liquor down the sink. Don't rant and rave . . . You have to detach yourself from the person who is an alcoholic and . . . save your own life."

Two of the most successful organizations helping families of alcoholics are Al-Anon, with half a million members, and its offshoot, Alateen, whose forty-five thousand teenage members are almost all children of alcoholics. Besides the "Three Cs" of Al-Anon, ("I didn't cause the alcoholism. I can't control it. I can't cure it.") Nan Robertson says there should be a fourth C: "I can change myself."

For many years, Alcoholics Anonymous did not encourage women to become members. Therefore, Al-Anon began because the wives of alcoholics felt a need for an organization in which they could voice the problems they experienced with their alcoholic husbands. During the 1940s, Bill Wilson, the co-founder of Alcoholics Anonymous, and his wife, Lois, traveled across the United States starting AA groups. A spin-off of their efforts was the formation of AA Family Groups, which adapted AA's recovery program to fit their needs. In 1950 Bill suggested Lois open an office in New York City, where families of alcoholics could come for help and get literature on alcoholism.

With the aid of Anne B., another wife of an alcoholic, Lois wrote to eighty-seven AA Family Groups, proposing to unify them under one organization separate from AA. Forty-eight groups responded. In 1951, Al-Anon, a contraction of Alcoholics Anonymous, was officially formed. Anne B. and Lois wrote *Purposes and Suggestions for Al-Anon Family Groups,* which emphasized focusing on oneself rather than on the alcoholic.

The first Al-Anon groups, composed mostly of wives of AA members, met either in each others' homes or in anterooms outside AA meetings. Their office equipment consisted of one typewriter and two drawers in a filing cabinet. Lois saved the cardboards from Bill's dry-cleaned shirts to stiffen the envelopes containing pamphlets mailed to Al-Anon groups around the United States. When someone phoned long distance asking for help, they'd look in an atlas for the nearest town to the caller holding an Al-Anon meeting. The caller felt grateful if the meeting were only four hundred miles away.

In the late 1950s, Al-Anon broke away from AA and became a separate organization. Headquarters were located on Manhattan's East 23rd Street.

In 1962 Al-Anon received much needed public-

A woman holds up a publicity poster of Alateen, a support group made up mostly of teenage children of alcoholics.

ity from an unexpected source: an article about the organization written by the advice columnist Ann Landers. Afterwards, four thousand letters poured into her office, and ten thousand letters flooded the Al-Anon office. Families of alcoholics were finally coming out of the closet. In 1966, Al-Anon published its official book, *Living with an Alcoholic* (the title was later changed to *Al-Anon Family Groups*). In 1985 Al-Anon established its World Service Office in New York's garment district.

As Al-Anon has grown, so has its membership—from unemployed housewives of alcoholic husbands, to husbands, parents, children, siblings, employers, and employees of alcoholics. Half its members are college educated and employed. More than a quarter hold professional or executive jobs. Al-Anon's purpose has changed from how to keep a marriage together and save the alcoholic family member, to individual recovery from the effects of living with an alcoholic. Membership is free, and the only requirement is that an important person in your life be an alcoholic.

In 1986, Al-Anon published its first videocassette. In it a member says, "I used to be a doormat for my husband. But anybody who goes to Al-Anon . . . learns to think for herself and become her own person. . . ." As quoted in Nan Robertson's book, "They [the family members] refuse to be some therapeutic tool to fix somebody else."

Today there are twenty-eight thousand Al-Anon groups worldwide, fifteen thousand in the United States. All groups meet at least once a week. Al-Anon Information Services, listed in phone books in every major U.S. city, provide locations of meetings near a caller's home. Of the many books and pamphlets Al-Anon publishes, the most popular is *One Day at a Time in Al-Anon* (ODAT). Small enough to fit into a pocket, it includes a blank page for every day of the year. At the top of each page is a quotation called, "Today's Reminder," which focuses on a specific topic, such as anger, blame, fear, or forgiveness. Underneath the "Reminder" members write their experiences and feelings of growth.

Al-Anon meetings last about an hour, and are held in churches, synagogues, or community centers. People sit around a table for intimate talks, or in an audience-type setting if there is a speaker. The philosophy is based upon Alcoholic Anonymous's Twelve Step Recovery Program. The first step says, "We admitted we were powerless over alcohol, that our lives had become unmanageable." To a nondrinker, this First Step might sound confusing. How can you be powerless over alcohol if you don't drink? As one member explained, "The First Step means that we are powerless over the person who drinks . . . We're powerless to make them stop, and we're not responsible for them becoming alcoholics, either, no matter what they say." And perhaps most important, a family member's recovery does not depend upon the alcoholic's recovery.

The meeting starts with someone reading the Al-Anon Preamble, which says that Al-Anon Family Groups are a fellowship of relatives and friends of alcoholics who share their experiences, strengths, and hope, in order to solve common problems. Another person welcomes new members, assuring them that everything said will be held in confidence.

Next the speaker for that particular meeting tells her story of what it was like to live with an alcoholic, and what she is doing now to help herself. For example, one woman told how she would promise herself, "I will not stop my tirade until I get through to him. . . ." She hid her husband's drinking from outsiders. "Everyone thought of us as the perfect little family. . . ." Then she stopped going out with friends. "If I went out, he might sneak out while I was gone . . . . I went from a self-sufficient, strong, happy person to a dependent, weak, miserable one."

When the speaker finishes, the floor is open to those who have something on their minds they'd like to talk about. Members offer suggestions. One woman said she used to constantly spy on her husband to see if he was drinking. If he were watching television, she'd think, "What's he got on the other side of the sofa? . . . Then I woke up one morning and I told myself, 'You're going to live this day as if you were living alone. He, at least, is watching TV. All I'm doing is watching him watch TV. Who has the problem?' "

One man in the group said, "I heard the word *detachment* a lot when I first came [to Al-Anon]. . . . Detachment means you've got to stop being a prison guard or nurse. I've stopped yelling at her, preaching at her. I've stopped . . . looking for the bottles she's hidden behind the books. . . ."

The meeting ends with the Al-Anon closing: "I would like to say that the opinions expressed here were strictly those of the person who gave them. Take what you liked and leave the rest. . . ."

Adult Children Of Alcoholics

Children of alcoholic parents carry their childhood emotional scars into adulthood. "When we were kids and our parents were drunk, it was our problem," a twenty-one-year-old daughter of an alcoholic said. "Somehow it seemed we should be super people and make our family healthy."

In the early 1980s a movement formed to help all children of alcoholics. Named Adult Children of Alcoholics (ACOAs) or more commonly, Children of Alcoholics (COAs), the movement started as a result of COAs feeling that their problems from having been raised by alcoholic parents were being neglected. (By 1988 there were an estimated seven million children under eighteen living in alcoholic homes in the United States, as well as twenty-one million adult children of alcoholics.)

In 1983 the National Association of Children of Alcoholics (NACOA) was founded in South Laguna, California, by a team of therapists, teachers, authors, and physicians. Their purpose was to establish "a network of information and caring for the sake of young, adolescent, and adult children of alcoholics everywhere." By 1986 there were 1,100 COA groups in the United States, and membership in NACOA totalled seven thousand.

COAs are raised by three rules which cause them severe emotional distress. Don't talk. Don't trust. Don't feel. According to poet Robert Bly, "Every child of an alcoholic receives the knowledge that the bottle is more important to the parent than he or she is." When these children grow up, although they have the intelligence of adults, they still have the wounded feelings of a child.

The COA movement first came to national attention with the 1983 publication of the book *Adult Children of Alcoholics,* by Janet Geringer Woititz, a human-relations counselor in Verona, New Jersey. Woititz wrote about how the traumas of growing up with an alcoholic parent affect the adult's behavior. She listed thirteen such adult behaviors, including

- difficulty finishing a project

- difficulty having fun

- difficulty having intimate relationships

- lying

- judging oneself too harshly

- overreacting to changes over which they have no control

- constantly seeking approval

- feeling they are different from other people

- being super-responsible, super-irresponsible, or extremely loyal, even though the other person does not deserve that loyalty

- acting without considering the consequences.

(74)

"We confuse love with pity," said one ACOA, "and tend to love people whom we can pity and rescue." COAs thus have a tendency to marry alcoholics because they've been conditioned to accept unacceptable behavior.

COAs experience daily terrors that most people do not experience in a lifetime. Young children, for example, are forced to ride in a car with a drunk driver, and have no one to tell of that horror. When asked, "How are you?" a child of an alcoholic will always say, "Fine." COAs feel guilty for their failure to save Mom or Dad from alcohol. "What did I do to get Dad to drinking like that?" they ask themselves. Or, "I tried to help, but it never worked. I really don't count much with them." Anger is expressed by statements like, "Why can't our house be like my friends'?" Or, "I can't wait till I get old enough to get out of this mess."

"Children of alcoholics are people who've been robbed of their childhood," says author Woititz. "I've seen five-year-olds running entire families." One eight-year-old awakened in the middle of the night to see her alcoholic mother shoot herself in the head. The child called 911, got her mother to the hospital, and saved her mother's life, all without the help of an adult.

Recent studies show that because COAs feel different from others, they develop a poor self-image, in which they closely resemble their alcoholic parents. COAs have a rage inside them that, if not dealt with in some form of therapy, goes repressed for years, usually to explode in adulthood in acts of violence.

Some children of alcoholics compensate for the attention they lack from their parents by becoming addicted to anything that will give them a sense of comfort. The child who compulsively overeats, or dresses to perfection, or abuses drugs are examples.

COAs are raised without ever seeing appropriately functioning parents. There are usually no family meals together since the alcoholic's drinking takes away his appetite. Because alcoholics are either out drinking or passed out at home, their children cannot count on help with school projects or homework. The parent may fly into a rage and throw things, often the child, across the room. Frequently the child is put in a foster home until the alcoholic parent recovers, which may take anywhere from a few months to years, resulting in feelings of no permanency in a child's life.

Just like husband and wives of alcoholics, COAs think they can stop their alcoholic parent from drinking by such devices as hiding the liquor, not disturbing that parent so he or she can rest, or by achieving good grades in school. These children try to keep everything in their lives under control.

Several other books about COAs have been published, notably *Another Chance,* by Sharon Wegscheider-Cruze, who coined four classic roles children of alcoholics play in order to take away attention from the alcoholic's troubles and give the children a sense of security:

- The Family Hero—usually the firstborn, he or she is a high achiever, always does what's right and puts others first

- The Scapegoat—appears hostile and defiant, but inside feels hurt and angry. He or she gets attention through negative behavior and is likely to be involved in alcohol or drugs later

- The Lost Child—is withdrawn, a loner, who will have a joyless adulthood

- The Mascot—fragile, immature, yet charming, the family clown.

"Life for these children," says author Woititz, "is a state of constant anxiety." Many pediatricians think there is a link between such anxiety and childhood ulcers, chronic nausea, sleeping problems, and eating disorders.

Treatment for adult children of alcoholics involves group therapy, in which they relive painful childhood experiences, this time acting out the anger and hurt at the alcoholic parent that they suppressed in childhood, which allows them to feel emotions they've kept locked up for years. One adult child of an alcoholic recalls, "I had to learn to re-parent myself to comfort the little girl inside me."

Acting out of unresolved childhood traumas and expressions of rage also occur at COA meetings, which are conducted similar to AA and Al-Anon meetings, in that members tell their stories and receive helpful suggestions from others. Jean, now in her forties, told of her father losing job after job because of his drinking until he just sat home all day drinking. He fantasized Jean's mother was seeing other men and beat her. When Jean got in his way, he picked her up and

*Adult children of alcoholics give each other
emotional and moral support during therapy.*

threw her against a wall, twice causing her to be hospitalized. "Nobody in my family spoke," she said. "We screamed."

Migs Woodside, of the COAs foundation, says that trained teachers can spot a COA in a crowded classroom. "Sometimes you can tell . . . by the fact that they never have their lunch money." Or "they suddenly pay attention when the teacher talks about drinking, and sometimes you can tell by their pictures." Their crayons tell their stories. Beer cans are the main picture in their drawings. Perhaps most tragic are the drawings which show a big stick figure tipping a beer can into the mouth of a little stick figure.

CHAPTER

5

TREATMENT FOR ALCOHOLICS

I hung up the phone, my boss's words still echoing in my ears. . . . . "Be in my office at exactly two o'clock, Tom. There's something we have to talk about." My shirt stuck to my back with sweat, and my stomach felt as if I'd chugged boric acid. I unlocked my bottom drawer. Time for a pick-me-up. As I pulled the vodka out, my hands shook so hard I had to hold the bottle between my knees while I unscrewed the cap. I took a giant swig. The vodka seared my insides, but my hands stopped shaking.

At five minutes of two, I took another slug and walked to Mr. Kilgore's office. When I stepped inside I almost keeled over. Sitting in the room were my boss, my wife, my two children, and a woman I didn't know.

She smiled. "I'm glad to meet you, Tom. I'm Sally Johnson. Mr. Kilgore and your family are very concerned about you. They each have something to say to you."

"What is this?" I glared at my wife. "If you've been telling lies about me again, I'll . . ."

"All you have to do is listen," Sally Johnson said. She turned to my wife. "You can start now, Nora."

"First I want to say I love you, Tom. But I can't live with you unless you stop drinking. The last time we had company you got so drunk you threw up at the dinner table. After everyone left, you ran around throwing things, screaming that monsters were chasing you. Then you started punching me. That's when Danny came home from his date."

"So that's it," I yelled. "You're trying to cover up for Danny. He probably came home soused, and you want to blame me. You've been against me for months."

"I'm scared of you when you're drunk," my wife said. "Worst of all, you don't remember doing anything hurtful. Let Danny tell you what happened when he came home."

My throat closed. I couldn't have hurt Nora. I loved her. I tried to remember, but my brain was one big cloud.

"You might have killed Mom if I hadn't come home when I did," Danny told me. "She was unconscious, and you kept punching her in the face. The only way I could get you to stop was to hit you with a lamp. I love you, too, Dad, but I swear to God, I wanted to kill you that night."

"You're lying," I shouted. "I ought to—"

"Let me finish," he cut in. "Remember my best

friend, Steve? He was with me that night and called the police. I talked the cops out of arresting you because I didn't want my dad locked up in some drunk tank. But I didn't do you any favors. Because two days ago you almost killed Debbie.''

"My friends won't come over anymore," Tom's daughter said. "Not since you drove us to the skating rink. You were drinking a Pepsi. But it wasn't Pepsi in that can. It was vodka. You drove so fast we got knocked all around the car. Then you ran a stop sign and a truck almost hit us. Now my friends call you a drunk."

"Debbie, honey, I didn't mean to hurt you." I rushed toward her, but she pushed me away. I backed up against the door, my legs buckling and my heart racing.

"So, Tom, " Mr. Kilgore said. "Even though you're one of my most competent employees, if you don't go to the alcoholic treatment center today, you're fired, as of now."

"I've made an appointment for you to be admitted to the alcoholic treatment center at four o'clock," my wife said. "Either we take you straight to the center, or you'll have to find somewhere else to live."

Guilt and pain tore me apart. How could I have hurt my family and not known it? I looked at each one of them. "I'll go wherever you say."

Breaking through the Barrier of Denial

Scenes like this are being played out across the United States every day. What Tom's family did is called "intervention." It is a technique developed in the early 1960s by Vernon Johnson, an Episcopal priest in Minneapolis, Minnesota, to force alcoholics into seeking treatment before their bodies deteriorated to the fatal stage of the disease.

Because the two main barriers to alcoholics' seeking treatment is their denial that a problem exists and their belief that there is no way for them to get well, in the past most alcoholics waited to get treatment until they "bottomed out"—meaning a personal crisis occurred that broke through their denial and forced them to admit their drinking was causing themselves and the people they cared about great pain. However, by the time the crisis occurred, alcohol had destroyed their minds and bodies so badly that many died in spite of treatment.

Vernon Johnson reasoned that if alcoholics could be made to "bottom out" before they reached the fatal stage, they would seek treatment before it was too late. Thus, through intervention, family, friends, and co-workers confront the alcoholic with specific incidents of how his or her drinking has caused pain, danger, or embarrassment in their lives. The confrontation becomes the "personal crisis" (the bottoming out), breaks through the drinker's denial, and forces the alcoholic to seek treatment.

The intervention is planned in advance. First everyone taking part meets with an alcoholism counselor to rehearse what they will say in a calm, loving manner, without anger or resentment, no matter how the alcoholic reacts.

Intervention is painful for everyone involved. An adult daughter of an alcoholic read her mother a letter

(83)

in which she told how she had seen her mother change "from the best friend I ever had to an unhappy and unreliable woman. The good parts of your character are being stolen away by alcohol. Don't let that bottle overtake your life." Another teenage daughter might have said she will no longer be embarrassed by her mother's drunken behavior when she brings friends home, and she is moving in with one of her friends.

Not all alcoholics go into the hospital for treatment. Some people use a hospital's outpatient services, which include alcohol counseling and individual and group therapy, while others enter detoxification centers, recovery homes, or halfway houses. And countless alcoholics have recovered only by attending Alcoholics Anonymous meetings regularly. There is no one way to recover from alcoholism.

Detoxification Centers

The purpose of a detoxification center is to help alcoholics get through withdrawal symptoms brought on by the body's reaction to the sudden cease of alcohol in the bloodstream. Withdrawal symptons include shaking hands, sleeplessness, sweating, depression, headache, weakness, vomiting, alcoholic seizure, and delirium tremens, (d.t.'s). As you recall, d.t.'s are "a state of mental confusion and clouded consciousness, resulting from intoxication or shock, and characterized by anxiety, tremors, hallucinations, delusions and incoherence."

An alcoholic seizure is similar to an epileptic seizure in that people become unconscious while their bodies are convulsed by muscle spasms. Consciousness returns in about three to five minutes, followed by a few hours of amnesia, in which patients do not know their names or where they are. Patients stay in detoxification centers about three or four days, after which they are referred to another facility for further treatment.

Whether medication is used to lessen the effects of withdrawal depends upon the center's policies. Experts disagree on the use of medication. Some argue that if withdrawal symptoms are not blocked out by drugs, this is the best time to reach the alcoholic, as his denial is at its weakest point. Other experts believe patients need not go through the pain of withdrawal when there are drugs to put patients to sleep during the most severe symptoms.

The severity of withdrawal pain is equal to the severity of the physical condition of the patient. For example, a drinker who stays sober during the day and only gets drunk at night probably will not need to go to a detoxification center to withdraw. A local office of the National Council on Alcoholism or Alcoholics Anonymous can recommend detoxification centers suited to an individual's needs.

Recovery from alcoholism is a step-by-step process. After detoxification, patients who immediately go home and continue life as before usually start drinking again within a short time, as they have not learned other ways besides drinking to deal with their problems. Therefore, the recommended procedure is to enter a recovery home or hospital treatment center after detoxification.

Recovery Homes

A recovery home, sometimes called an Intermediate Care Facility, is similar to a recovery room in a hospital in that it is a quiet, supervised place for people to begin recovering from an illness. During a patient's stay, normally from one to three months, they attend lectures, tapes, and movies on addictive drinking, individual and group counseling sessions, and AA meetings. Upon dismissal, patients are encouraged to keep attending AA meetings on the outside. The slogan in recovery homes is "You alone can do it, but you can't do it alone." This means that the staff gives the alcoholic tools for recovery, but it is up to the alcoholic to use them to stay sober.

Hospital Treatment Centers

There are two types of hospital alcoholic treatment facilities: the state-run alcoholic ward, and the privately run alcoholic treatment hospital. Since for years alcoholism was considered a form of mental illness, state-run wards at first consisted of one room in a mental hospital. Patients were locked inside the ward until their withdrawal symptoms stopped. Then they were discharged. The alcoholic ward's growth to entire floors devoted to alcoholic rehabilitation was a direct result of new treatments for the mentally ill, such as medications which provided an alternative to hospitalization.

The decrease in mental patients left so many unoccupied hospital beds that these hospitals lost money. Thus, mental hospitals were motivated to expand their

*An alcohol/drug counselor discusses
the effects of chemical dependency
with recovering addicts.*

services to include patients with other diseases such as alcoholism. Today, life on an alcoholic ward is filled with many indoor and outdoor activities. Weekend passes are worked into the treatment schedule to allow alcoholics to adjust to living in the outside world before they are dismissed.

Patients are assigned to a specific therapist who is responsible for conducting group and individual therapy, as well as granting unsupervised use of hospital grounds and home leaves. Most hospital treatment programs require patients to attend films and lectures on the physical, emotional, and mental damages of alcoholism, as well as AA meetings (either in or out of the hospital), and to complete lesson assignments from AA literature.

Therapy consists of first persuading the patients to admit they are alcoholics. Eventually, discussions center around such issues as how early childhood experiences influenced later drinking problems; how to deal with stress that leads to renewed drinking; and how staying sober is the way to achieve goals and lead productive lives. In addition, after-care treatment is discussed, including attending alcohol clinics, psychotherapy, and AA meetings.

Private hospitals offer practically the same alcohol recovery programs as state-run hospitals. Private facilities began to flourish in the United States in 1982, after former U.S. president Gerald Ford's wife Betty publicly admitted she had received treatment for alcoholism, then opened the Betty Ford Center in Rancho Mirage, California. Since then other celebrities, such as actresses Elizabeth Taylor and Drew Barrymore, and baseball pitcher Bob Welch, have publicly told of their alcohol and drug addictions, thus serving as role models for countless people who otherwise might have been too ashamed to seek treatment.

Private substance-abuse hospitals are under the direction of a physician or psychiatrist and staffed by registered nurses with psychiatric training. Because of the high specialization of the staff, the cost to patients is high. A twenty-eight-day stay can cost up to $15,000, or more, compared to about $10,000 for the same time in a recovery home, or $3000 for four hours of therapy and education once a week for a month in an outpatient program. Around ten thousand companies in the United States now have employee-assistance programs to help alcohol and drug abusers.

Ninety-five percent of in-patient hospitals use a 28-day educational program about alcohol abuse developed in 1949 at Hazelden Clinic in Minnesota, one of the pioneers in hospital treatment for alcoholics. Group therapy focuses on dispelling the alcoholic's self-delusions about drinking by teaching them how excessive drinking destroys the mind and body, and by stressing that the only way to recover is to stop drinking. Children and teenage patients attend classes held in the hospital so they can keep up with their education. Their families are encouraged to become involved in their recovery by attending family therapy sessions in which such issues as love, dependency, anger, and trust are discussed.

Antabuse and the Aversion Therapy

Frequently, as an added incentive to "stay dry," doctors prescribe the medication Antabuse (disulfiram).

Antabuse is a pill which makes the body violently allergic to alcohol in any form, including non-prescription drugs that contain alcohol, such as cough medicines, aftershave lotions, and mouthwash. If a person drinks alcohol while on Antabuse, violent reactions occur, such as a red or purple skin rash, stomach cramps, vomiting, headaches, and severe rises and drops in temperature and blood pressure. According to people who drank while on Antabuse, the result was so painful they wanted to die.

Antabuse is not a cure for alcoholism. Rather, it is a strong incentive not to drink. As one recovering alcoholic said, "Before I took Antabuse . . . I had to decide fifty times a day whether I was going to give up and drink or keep hanging in there. This constant battle kept interrupting everything I was trying to do. Then I started Antabuse. . . . I still wanted a drink just as often, but with that stuff in me, I knew I didn't have to decide fifty times a day anymore."

In addition, it takes five days after stopping Antabuse for the drug to leave the body, thus to be able to drink again without violent side effects. Therefore, people who stop taking the pill usually try the other methods of stress relief they learned in treatment before giving in to drinking. When alcoholics realize they made it through a stressful time without taking a drink, they usually decide to take Antabuse again.

Another treatment for alcoholism is aversion therapy, used by Schick Shadel, a program practiced in California, Texas, and Washington. Started as early as 1942, aversion therapy consists of injecting the alcoholic with a drug that causes nausea and vomiting, then giving that person a drink. If this method is repeated over and over, the person develops a severe negative association with alcohol, eventually recoiling even at the smell and sight of a drink.

Another form of aversion therapy consists of controlled electric shocks, in which the patients are fitted to electrodes and receive a shock every time they take a drink. Another innovative approach is videotaping alcoholics while on a drunken binge, then playing back the tape when they are sober to show them how they behave while drunk.

On the road to recovery, alcoholics go through specific stages, each with its temptation to drink. Early on, it may be hard to cope with withdrawal. Later, the patient may have trouble redeveloping a normal family and social life. Finally, there is a period when alcoholics no longer fear drinking as they once did. The solution is to help recovering alcoholics identify and face problems before they get so out of hand that a drink seems the only answer.

Halfway Houses

Halfway houses are places for alcoholics who are half way to recovery. The house is usually staffed by former alcoholics, and the residents do the cooking, cleaning, and other chores. Residents are usually expected to hold jobs outside the house. Except for church-affiliated halfway houses, the treatment program relies on AA's Twelve Step recovery program. In some halfway houses AA meetings are held every day, and attendance is required. The residents form groups to discuss their former drinking habits and problems staying sober. The idea is that individual sobriety is strengthened through the group's resolve to stay sober.

In some areas there are quarterway, halfway, and three-quarterway houses. In the quarterway house, after the first few days residents are allowed to attend outside AA meetings and are given day and weekend passes as the staff feels they can handle being on their own without drinking. Residents may not hold outside jobs. Because these houses are supported by state or county funds, room and board are usually free. Other times the house charges according to the individual's ability to pay.

In three-quarterway houses, there is only a limited recovery program, and all residents have outside jobs, with complete freedom to come and go. The basic purpose of halfway houses is to create a protected environment for recovering alcoholics where they can find friendship, education about alcohol addiction, and emotional support along the road to recovery. As in all alcohol recovery programs, the main goal is to reach a stage of renewed self-esteem, at which time the alcoholic is ready to return to normal life in the community.

Skid Row Houses

Skid Row houses for alcoholics developed from religious mission houses, or "soup kitchens," which were located in poor neighborhoods and staffed by volunteers who fed unemployed, homeless men. The staff believed that alcoholics were sinners who needed religious salvation. Today salvation still plays an important role in Skid Row houses, as both work and prayer are the mode of treatment. The houses are run by different religious denominations, and most are patterned after the Salvation Army's Harbor Light Program, the largest system of voluntary service for alcoholic Skid Row men. Harbor Light agencies, supported by the United Fund, are located in almost every large city in the United States and Canada.

The residents live dormitory style, food is served cafeteria style, and the residents themselves do the housecleaning. No Harbor Light House permits AA meetings on the premises, as they believe that formal religious services and seeking salvation are the ways to sobriety. Harbor Light does offer group therapy in which residents talk about their problems. After a week's stay, residents are urged to find jobs outside the house. Most Harbor Lights have an employment service for menial jobs, such as housecleaning and passing out handbills.

The quality and cost of each alcoholic treatment facility varies. The National Council on Alcoholism (NCA), the County Health Department, or a local AA office are the best sources of referral. Their numbers can be found in the phone book, or by calling telephone information.

Forgiveness and Spiritual Recovery

In order to recover from alcoholism, not only must alcoholics stop drinking permanently, but they must also regain enough self-esteem to cope with life situations without resorting to alcohol. Therefore, alcoholic recovery programs must treat the whole person — physically, mentally, emotionally, and spiritually.

Whereas detoxification treats the person physically, lectures and films begin the mental treatment. Patients learn how alcohol abuse affects all the body organs. Emotionally, patients learn how their defense systems have rationalized their drinking and made them lose touch with reality through memory loss. They learn that emotional pain occurs whenever their behavior is contrary to their values.

When patients fully believe that drinking, instead of giving them freedom from pain, has instead caused them even greater pain, then their defense barriers crumble, and they start to believe that quitting drinking provides the real freedom from pain that they seek. They realize that it isn't a new self they need, but rather their old self with a new way of behaving.

Spiritually, patients learn to forgive themselves and accept forgiveness from others for their abusive behavior. Acceptance of forgiveness is a vital step to recovery, as it means the alcoholics have forgiven themselves, and thus have accepted themselves as they are.

It is as difficult for codependents to forgive the alcoholic as it is for alcoholics to accept forgiveness from their codependents. Codependents must first acknowledge their anger and resentment toward the alcoholic for the pain he or she has caused them. They must then express that anger and resentment, and finally let go and forgive. Forgiving someone who hurts you deeply is not easy. It forces codependents to accept their own failings and destructive attitudes as well as value the need for similar forgiveness from the alcoholic. In order to be real, forgiveness also means restoring trust in the relationship, even if that should mean exposing the codependents to the risk of getting themselves hurt again.

The rewards of forgiveness are a restored self-image for both the alcoholic and the codependent, and a renewed closeness. In families where recovery is successful, parents and children experience greater love for each other through their understanding and trust of each other. A truly honest communication between families develops.

Stages of Recovery

There are four stages of recovery that alcoholics typically work through. First is admission that they have a disease called alcoholism, or in medical terms, "acute chronic alcoholism." The second stage is compliance, in which patients' attitudes change from doubting the seriousness of their condition to believing their disease is fatal if they continue drinking.

The third stage is called acceptance, which means making an honest commitment to take personal responsibility for their recovery. In group therapy, for example, no one is allowed to try to change another alcoholic. Instead, whenever an alcoholic uses a rationalized defense to explain his behavior, that defense is called to his attention so that he becomes aware of how he is acting. Thus, patients *heal themselves* by recognizing when they are using defense systems that make them lose touch with reality. Patients during the acceptance stage start to care again not only about themselves, but about others as well.

The fourth stage of recovery is called surrender, in which patients are self-accepting, loving, and willing to risk close relationships again. Patients now change their view of sobriety from an easy path, expressed by such statements as, "There is no way I will ever drink again," to a realization that they will need help staying sober, expressed by such statements as, "When I leave this hospital, you better believe I'm going to stick as close to AA as I can get."

Patients are now ready to be discharged into an outpatient program of rehabilitation. Ideally, this involves a two-year period of weekly family therapy, plus weekly, if not more often, attendance at AA meetings for the alcoholic, and Al-Anon and Alateen meetings for codependents.

Many treatment facilities suggest that upon discharge the patient attend ninety AA meetings in the next ninety days and then begin regular attendance in an AA group, usually going two or three times a week.

Perhaps most frustrating for alcoholics and family members is that there is no guaranteed recovery program for alcoholism. Studies show that only 15 percent to 20 percent of alcoholics receive any treatment at all, and only 12 percent to 25 percent of patients completing a treatment program stay "on the wagon" for three years. Experts say that if alcoholism treatment is to have more than an average chance to succeed, then the entire family must be treated as well.

Alcohol addicts may also abuse other drugs. Students have been known to mix pills and liquor to get them through the eve of a big exam.

Complicating recovery is the increased combination of alcohol with another drug, such as tranquilizers, as was the case with former First Lady Betty Ford. Known as "cross addiction," researchers estimate that between 40 percent and 75 percent of people in treatment programs are multiple-substance abusers. Multiple abusers are more difficult to treat, as they often admit to abusing one drug, but hide the fact they are abusing tranquilizers or alcohol as well. Substance abuse counselors try to teach these people that abstinence means not taking any mood-altering drug, whether it comes in a bottle or in pill form.

Despite all the treatments available to alcoholics, most experts agree that the single most effective source of treatment is Alcoholics Anonymous. Today, with more than thirty-three thousand AA groups in existence, it is hard to believe that this world-famous international organization was started by two drunks in Akron, Ohio.

CHAPTER

6

ALCOHOLICS ANONYMOUS

God grant me the serenity
To accept the things I cannot change;
Courage to change the things I can;
And wisdom to know the difference.
—The Serenity Prayer
of Alcoholics Anonymous,
attributed to American
theologian Reinhold Niebuhr.

Saturday, May 11, 1935. Bill Wilson, an unemployed stockbroker, paced across the lobby of the Mayflower Hotel in Akron, Ohio. He was dying for a drink. Bill had traveled to Ohio from Brooklyn, New York, to convince some businessmen to invest in one of his "great" deals. But he had been turned down. Defeated, alone in a strange city, and missing his wife Lois, Bill heard laughter float out of the hotel bar, and felt it wrap itself around him, pulling him toward his old surefire cure for loneliness—booze.

Bill headed for the bar, then stopped. He pictured how his life had been for the past seventeen years: hands shaking so violently every morning that he needed a gin and a beer to eat breakfast; hallucinations and blackouts while he rode the subway drinking a bottle of gin and frightening other passengers with his gibberish.

While Lois worked at Macy's Department Store, Bill had either panhandled or stolen money from her purse to buy booze. He'd come home roaring drunk, screaming at Lois, storming around their house, kicking out door panels. Once he even threw a sewing machine at Lois. He barely ate and he was forty pounds underweight. He once fell down the stairs and passed out in his own vomit. Bill Wilson was then thirty-nine years old.

If he went back on the bottle, he probably wouldn't make it to his fortieth birthday. In December 1934, Bill had entered a drying-out hospital for the fourth time. Three experiences occurred there that gave him an honest desire to stop drinking. First, an old classmate, also an alcoholic, visited Bill and told him about the Oxford Group, an international movement that preached a return to the simple faith of the early Christians in order to live a moral Christian life.

Although the Oxford Group was not established to help any particular disease, its philosophy helped Bill's classmate stop drinking. The program included surrendering his life to God, having recognized that he couldn't run it himself; trying to be honest with himself, making amends to people he had hurt; trying to give himself to others without asking anything in return; and finally, prayer.

When his friend left, Bill fell into a deep depression. He thought, I'll do anything, anything for release. . . . If there be a God, let Him show Himself! Then, according to Bill, a blinding white light suddenly entered the room and penetrated his body, filling him with "a joy beyond description. I felt lifted up, as though the great clean wind of a mountaintop blew through and through. . . ." From that moment on, Bill started believing in God.

The third incident came from Dr. William Duncan Silkworth, the neurologist who ran the hospital. Dr. Silkworth gave Bill a feeling of self-worth not given to alcoholics of the 1930s, when drunks were thought to be morally defective, weak-willed lushes who were locked in insane asylums. At that time, the common treatment for alcoholics was to use large doses of narcotics, or to purge them with castor oil. But Dr. Silkworth believed that alcoholism was caused by a physical "allergy" to liquor, and a compulsion to drink over which alcoholics had no control.

Whether Bill experienced a true religious experience, or a hallucination caused by withdrawal from alcohol, is not known for sure. However, when he left the hospital on December 18, 1934, Bill Wilson never took another drink in his life. He became obsessed with helping other drunks. Bill found that talking to other alcoholics about his own drinking problem kept him from taking that longed-for drink. To further help his sobriety, Bill attended Oxford Group meetings.

Now, on this Saturday in May, Bill turned from the hotel bar and walked to a church directory at the end of the lobby, hoping to find the phone number of a clergyman that he could talk to who was a member of the Oxford Group. After many phone calls, an Episcopal minister put Bill in touch with Henrietta Sieberling, whose ex-husband was the son of the founder of Goodyear Tire and Rubber Company. Bill's first words to her were, "I'm from the Oxford Group, and I'm a rum hound from New York."

Henrietta Sieberling attended the Oxford Group for comfort after her husband abandoned her and their three children. There she became friends with fifty-five-year-old Dr. Robert Holbrook Smith, an alcoholic proctologist (a doctor who treats diseases related to the rectum and anus), whose medical practice was disintegrating due to his drinking. Both Henrietta and Dr. Smith's wife, Anne, had tried every means to get "Dr. Bob," as he was called, to quit drinking. Now when Bill Wilson asked Henrietta if she knew a drunk he could talk to in order to stay sober himself, Henrietta thought, This is like manna from heaven. She arranged for the two men to meet at her house.

Bill and Dr. Bob talked for six hours. Bill told his story of taking his first drink while in the army during World War I. After the war, he became a stockbroker and his drinking increased while he entertained clients. Finally he'd hit rock bottom along with the stock market crash of 1929, which ended his career.

Dr. Bob told about how he'd started drinking while attending Dartmouth College. "Drinking seemed to be a major extracurricular activity," he said. In medical school his drinking increased and he "got the shakes." During final exams he turned in three completely blank test booklets. He finally received his M.D. at age thirty-one. During prohibition, physicians were allowed unlimited quantities of grain alcohol for medicinal purposes. Dr. Bob would pick a name from the phone book, then fill out a prescription for alcohol.

Unlike Bill Wilson, Dr. Bob was a secret drinker. He hid bottles over doorjambs, in the coal bin, and in cracks in the cellar tile. But like Bill Wilson, after every binge he promised never to drink again, and never kept his promises. The hospital administrators put him on warning, his practice dwindled, and his family frequently lived on potato soup, bread, and milk.

When the two men emerged from Henrietta Sieberling's library, Dr. Bob had been won over to Bill Wilson's method of talking to other drunks to stay sober, and Alcoholics Anonymous was born. Years later, Dr. Bob wrote of that meeting: " . . . he [Bill Wilson] was the first living human with whom I had ever talked, who knew what he was talking about in regard to alcoholism from actual experience. In other words, he talked my language. . . ."

A Fellowship of Two

The pattern of recovery that these two men set—a fellowship of two—has been followed by millions of drunks all over the world. There had to be two foun-

(103)

Bill Wilson (left) and Robert "Dr. Bob" Holbrook Smith, the founders of Alcoholics Anonymous

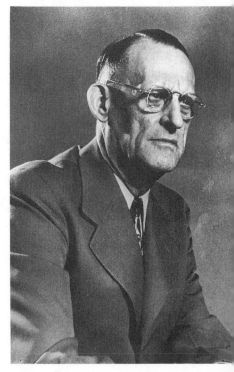

ders of AA, because the essence of the program is one person telling his story to another as honestly as he knows how.

In June 1935, Dr. Bob went on one last drinking binge at the American Medical Association convention in Atlantic City, New Jersey. It took him three days to get sober. He had an operation scheduled for the third day. On the way to the hospital, Bill gave Dr. Bob a bottle of beer to steady his nerves. Alcoholics Anonymous marks its beginning on that day, June 10, 1935, when Dr. Bob took his last drink.

Determined to help other alcoholics become sober, the two men started working with drunk patients at the City Hospital in Akron. Next, they started recruiting alcoholics off the streets. Carloads of drunks would arrive every night for meetings at Dr. Bob's house. Anne would make pots of coffee as the men sat in the living room telling their stories. This "telling your own story" is the major part of every AA meeting today.

On August 11, 1938, Dr. Bob and Bill established a charitable organization called the Alcoholic Foundation, based in New York City. Bill wrote a textbook to be used by members as a guide to sobriety. Called "The Big Book" by members, it included Bill's recovery program called "The Twelve Steps." The steps called for alcoholics to admit their shortcomings and powerlessness over alcohol, and encouraged them to develop a "spiritual awakening" to a power greater than themselves. The Twelve Steps has been so successful that other addiction groups, such as Al-Anon, Alateen, Narcotics Anonymous, Overeaters Anonymous, and Gamblers Anonymous, have patterned their recovery programs after them.

In 1941 Alcoholics Anonymous received the break it needed to succeed. The *Saturday Evening Post,* a weekly magazine read by more than three million Americans, ran an article about the AA. Membership quadrupled from two thousand to eight thousand, and AA changed from a ridiculed group of skid row bums to a respected organization. By 1944, there were ten thousand members in 360 AA groups.

Along with the Twelve Steps program, Bill wrote the "Twelve Traditions," which sets forth guidelines for AA group behavior. Perhaps the most important tradition is anonymity. Members introduce themselves by first names only, and nothing that goes on at meetings is discussed with outsiders. Another tradition is that each group functions independently of AA national headquarters in New York.

The fear of corruption by wealth, property, power, and politics is as strong an AA tenet today as when the organization was created. For example, AA does not become involved in political or religious issues, charges no dues, owns no real estate, will not accept gifts of property or money from non-members, and will not accept over $1,000 a year from any one member. In addition, no member may leave more than $1,000 to AA in their wills.

In July 1950, AA held its first international convention. Dr. Bob, then seventy-one and dying of cancer, told the three thousand members in attendance to keep in mind the simplicity of the program and that "our Twelve Steps, when simmered down to the last, resolve themselves into the words *love* and *service*." On November 16, 1950, Dr. Bob died. Bill Wilson died on January 24, 1971, after a long bout with emphysema (a lung disease). In keeping with AA's anonymous tradition, neither Bill Wilson's nor Dr. Bob's tombstone mentions AA.

Today, Alcoholics Anonymous has grown from its original one hundred male, white, middle-class members (women were discouraged from attending meetings at first, the belief being that "nice" women don't get drunk) to nearly two million members in 63,000 groups in 114 countries. Women now form one-third of AA's membership, and there are increasing numbers of young people joining AA. There are even groups for the deaf, in which members speak in sign language.

Meetings are held in synagogues, churches, homes, community centers, hospitals, offices, corporation boardrooms, schools, ships at sea, and even prisons. There are 45,000 AA members in prisons today. A new member typically has a sponsor (someone who has been sober in AA for at least one year and acts as a "big brother or sister,") helping new members work through the Twelve Steps at small workshops. A sponsor is always available to talk or come over when the new member needs emotional support. For "loners"—people too sick or who live too far to attend meetings, staffers edit the newsletter *Loners-Internationalists Meeting,* in which people exchange their thoughts, problems, fears, and joys.

What Is an AA Meeting Like?

Neither preaching on the ravages of alcohol nor putting down of other members for their past drunken behavior occurs at AA meetings. The atmosphere is welcoming and supportive. As members say, "Yesterday is a closed chapter; tomorrow's events are yet to be written." When you walk into an AA meeting, you'll see a big coffee pot and some refreshments. Help yourself. It's free. Another table holds AA pamphlets and copies of the Big Book.

At the scheduled time (AA meetings always start on time and last no longer than an hour and a half) the chairperson for that evening welcomes everyone and reads the AA Preamble, then asks if anyone is celebrating a "birthday." A birthday in AA is a period of time a member has been sober. Birthdays usually occur at one month, three months, six months, one year, and then yearly thereafter. Members are given "chips" saying, for example, "One month sober." For a member's one-year birthday, he or she may be given a birthday cake. Everyone applauds the birthday persons.

Next a speaker usually talks for about twenty minutes about how they became alcoholics and how they stopped drinking. After the speech, the "hat is passed" to pay for use of the room, coffee, and refreshments. No one has to give anything, and the most anyone gives is one dollar.

There is a ten-minute coffee break, after which the floor is open to those who have something they

A speaker addresses Alcoholics Anonymous members at a meeting. The wall posters behind him refer to the AA program of recovery, which consists of twelve steps, and the organization's twelve traditions.

want to talk about, such as their jobs, how they over-
came the temptation to take a drink, good or bad events
happening in their lives, or their fears of slipping "off
the wagon." Members offer suggestions, such as
strenuous physical activity, calling an AA member,
or not going anywhere they used to while drinking. A
special way members help each other stay sober is
"telephone therapy." Whenever a member feels the
urge to drink is too strong to handle alone, he or she
phones another member, anytime day or night, and
they talk until the urge passes.

In addition to closed meetings, where only alcoholics may attend, there are open meetings where
friends and families are welcome. Open meetings may
have three speakers and a leader who tells some of
his story. There is no open discussion from the floor.
Open meetings give families a chance to see what their
relatives do at AA meetings, as well as newcomers a
chance to "test the waters" without taking part in the
drama that goes on during floor discussions.

Perhaps the major reason why Alcoholics Anonymous works is that instead of preaching a lifetime of
sobriety, an overwhelming thought for most alcoholics, AA reduces sobriety to a manageable concept:
Don't drink, one day at a time. The theory is that
most alcoholics can get through one day without alcohol. However, if that is too long a time period, AA
says tell yourself you won't drink one hour or one
minute at a time. If you can get through that first
minute, tell yourself you won't drink for the next
minute. Finally you'll be able to say, "I won't drink,
one day at a time," and mean it.

If a person is shy about attending their first meeting, they can phone the local AA office, and a member will take them to the meeting, introduce them around, and make sure they feel comfortable.

A thirty-five-year-old man said, "At my first meeting I was amazed to hear all these people talking about fears and problems that I had and had never talked to anybody about. I felt . . . these people . . . had come through the mill that I had." Another woman, age thirty-two, said, "At my first meeting, my hands were shaking like a leaf . . . Then a woman asked me if I wanted a cup of coffee. I panicked because I couldn't hold the cup without spilling it. She looked in my eyes and said, 'I'll hold it for you.' When I looked in her eyes, I knew she understood."

Fighting the Disease
of Alcoholism

Today, while scientists study genetic causes of alcoholism and search for preventions and cures, other individuals and organizations have started non-medical programs to deal with the disease. One program, called Teen Saferides, sponsored by the Boy Scouts of America, now has five hundred offices in the United States. Teenagers who are too drunk to drive home phone a special number, and a pair of teen volunteers equipped with an emergency kit pick them up and drive them home. In keeping with the group's policy of confidentiality, no names are asked or written down. Saferides is open from 10 P.M. until 2 A.M. every Friday and Saturday nights. Fifteen adult supervisors

These two young volunteers work for Teen Saferides. They provide escort services to teenagers too intoxicated to drive home by themselves.

help answer the phones, while fifty unpaid teen volunteers, who have received fifteen hours of training in self-defense and medical emergencies, work four-hour shifts.

Other organizations such as Mothers Against Drunk Driving (MADD), and Students Against Drunk Driving (SADD), are pushing the government to pass stricter drunk driving laws. Besides getting the legal drinking age pushed up to twenty-one in all states except Wyoming, another result of their efforts is the establishment of more traffic checkpoints where drivers suspected of being drunk are tested on hand-to-nose coordination. Tuscarawas County in Ohio puts bright orange plates on cars of drivers with suspended licenses. Twenty-two states now permit police officers to automatically lift the driver's license of anyone who flunks a Breathalyzer test or refuses to take one. And seventeen states impose mandatory license suspensions for first-time offenders convicted in court of drunk driving.

In addition, eight states are experimenting with devices that keep drunk drivers from turning on their car engines. Attached to the ignition system, these "interlocks" have a built-in microprocessor that takes a breath print. If the interlock picks up any traces of alcohol, or if the driver does not use it, the engine will not start. Some states require marks on offenders' driver's licenses that say they are permitted to drive only with the interlocks.

Many colleges have started alcohol programs featuring lectures and discussions on the hazards of drinking. A voluntary alcohol awareness organization

*Reading about the dangers of alcoholism
is one way that young people
can fight the deadly disease.*

called Bacchus, begun at the University of Florida in 1976, has now spread to 280 campuses. The University of California at Berkeley has banned drinking in public areas of dormitories and at fraternity and sorority rush parties.

Marguerite T. Saunders, director of the Division of Alcoholism and Alcohol Abuse, suggests four things to help young people with alcohol use and abuse:

- teach everyone that alcohol is a drug and that the only acceptable choice for young people is not to use it;

- develop a strategy that encompasses the home, community, school, and workplace to prevent alcohol and drug abuse;

- stop alcohol promotions aimed at children and young people, including those on college campuses;

- provide treatment for all young people needing help.

Meanwhile, countless recovering alcoholics, remembering their humiliating behavior and the deteriorated shape their bodies and minds were in while drunk, have found strength in this one thought: There is nothing so bad that can happen to me that a drink won't make worse.

APPENDIX A
"ARE YOU AN ALCOHOLIC?"
CHECKLIST

(ANSWER YES OR NO TO EACH QUESTION)

1. Do you occasionally drink heavily after a disappointment, a quarrel, or when the boss, parent, or teacher gives you a hard time?
2. When you have trouble or feel under pressure, do you always drink more heavily than usual?
3. Have you noticed that you are able to handle more liquor than you did when you were first drinking?
4. Did you ever wake up on the morning after and discover that you could not remember part of the evening before, even though your friends tell you that you did not pass out?
5. When drinking with other people, do you try to have a few extra drinks when others will not know it?
6. Are there certain occasions when you feel uncomfortable if alcohol is not available?

7. Have you recently noticed that when you begin drinking you are in more of a hurry to get the first drink than you used to be?
8. Do you sometimes feel a little guilty about your drinking?
9. Are you secretly irritated when your family or friends discuss your drinking?
10. Have you recently noticed an increase in the frequency of your memory "blackouts"?
11. Do you often find that you wish to continue drinking after your friends say they have had enough?
12. Do you usually have a reason for the occasions when you drink heavily?
13. When you are sober, do you often regret things you have done or said while drinking?
14. Have you tried switching brands or following different plans for controlling your drinking?
15. Have you often failed to keep the promises you have made to yourself about controlling or cutting down on your drinking?
16. Have you ever tried to control your drinking by changing jobs, or moving to a new location?
17. Do you try to avoid family or close friends while you are drinking?
18. Are you having an increasing number of financial and work problems?
19. Do more people seem to be treating you unfairly without good reason?
20. Do you eat very little or irregularly when you are drinking?
21. Do you sometimes have the shakes in the morning and find that it helps to have a little drink?

22. Have you recently noticed that you cannot drink as much as you once did?
23. Do you sometimes stay drunk for several days at a time?
24. Do you sometimes feel very depressed and wonder whether life is worth living?
25. Sometimes after periods of drinking, do you see or hear things that aren't there?
26. Do you get terribly frightened after you have been drinking heavily?

Answers:

The National Council on Alcoholism says if you answered yes to *any* of these questions, you have some symptoms that may indicate alcoholism. If you answered yes to the following questions, it indicates you are in the following stages of alcoholism:

Questions 1–8: Early Stage
Questions 9–21: Middle Stage
Questions 22–26: The beginning of the Final Stage

APPENDIX B
ALCOHOLISM HELP
ORGANIZATIONS
AND HOTLINES

Alcoholics Anonymous—National Headquarters
P.O. Box 459
Grand Central Station
New York, NY 10163
(212) 686-1100
(Or look in your local telephone directory for the number of your local AA office, for help. They will also provide locations of meetings in your area.)

Al-Anon Family Group Headquarters
P.O. Box 862
Midtown Station
New York, NY 10018-0862
Twenty-four-hour answering service: (800) 356-9996
and in New York and Canada, phone: (212) 302-7240
(Or look in your local telephone directory under Al-Anon Family Groups for information on Al-Anon and Alateen and the locations of local meetings.)

National Council on Alcoholism
12 West 21st Street, 7th Floor
New York, NY 10010
Twenty-four-hour, seven-day hotline: (800) NCA-CALL (622-2255)

National Clearinghouse for Alcohol and Drug Information
P.O. Box 2345
Rockville, MD 20852
(301) 468-2600
(Will supply list of treatment programs and information on specific alcohol and drug problems.)

National Association of Addiction Treatment Providers
22082 Michelson Drive, Suite 304
Irvine, CA 92715
(Provides lists of and information on alcoholism rehabilitation centers.)

Adult Children of Alcoholics
Suite 200
2522 West Sepulveda Blvd.
Torrance, CA 90505
(213) 534-1815

National Association for Children of Alcoholics
Suite 201
31706 Coast Highway
South Laguna, CA 92677
(714) 499-3889

Children of Alcoholics Foundation
200 Park Avenue, 31st Floor
New York, NY 10166

National Institute on Alcohol Abuse and Alcoholism
5600 Fishers Lane
Rockville, MD 20857

National Institute on Drug Abuse Helpline
(800) 662-HELP (4357) or (800) 843-4971
(Nine A.M. to 3:00 P.M. Eastern Standard Time, Monday to Friday; 12:00 P.M. to 3:00 P.M. Eastern Standard Time, Saturday and Sunday.)

Covenant House
9-Line (Twenty-four-hour, seven-day crisis hotline for runaway youths.) (800) 999-9999

ASAP Treatment Center
Twenty-four-hour, seven-day hotline (800) 367-2727

Hazelden Pioneer House
Hotline (612) 559-2022
(Nine A.M. to 5:30 P.M. Eastern Standard Time, Monday to Friday.)

FOR FURTHER READING

Ackerman, Robert. *Let Go and Grow*. Pompano Beach, FL: Health Communications, Inc., 1988.

Alcoholics Anonymous Publications, Inc. *Twelve Steps and Twelve Traditions*. New York: 1952.

Black, Claudia. *It Will Never Happen To Me*. Denver, CO: M.A.C. Publishers, 1981.

Bly, Robert. *Family Secrets*. New York: Harper & Row, 1987.

Doris, Michael. *The Broken Cord*. New York: Harper & Row, 1989.

The Hazelden Foundation. *Codependent No More: How To Stop Controlling Others and Start Caring For Yourself*. New York: Harper & Row, 1987.

Kritsberg, Wayne. *The Adult Children of Alcoholics Syndrome: From Discovery to Recovery.* Pompano Beach, FL: Health Communications, Inc., 1985.

Maxwell, Ruth. *Breakthrough: What To Do When Alcoholism or Chemical Dependency Hits Close To Home.* New York: Ballantine Books, 1986.

Moore, Jean. *Roads to Recovery.* New York: Macmillan, 1986. Lists and describes hundreds of treatment facilities in the U.S.

Robertson, Nan. *Getting Better: Inside Alcoholics Anonymous.* New York: William Morrow, 1988.

Wegscheider-Cruze, Sharon. *Another Chance: Hope and Health for the Alcoholic Family.* Palo Alto, CA: Science & Behavior Books, Inc., 1981.

Woititz, Janet Geringer. *Adult Children of Alcoholics.* Pompano Beach, FL: Health Communications, Inc., 1983.

INDEX

Numbers in *italics* indicate photo captions.

Adoption studies, 31, 32–33
Adult Children of Alcoholics (ACOAs), 73
Al-Anon, 63, 65, 67–73, 96, 105
Alateen, 67, *69*, 96, 105
Alcohol:
    history of, 22–24
    physiological effects of, 35–40
Alcoholics Anonymous (AA), 14, 18, 23–24, 42, 59, 67–68, 71, 84, 86, 88, 91–92, 93, 96, 98, 99–111
    birth of, 99–105
    meetings of, 108–11, *109*
    Twelve step program of, 71, 91, 105–7

Alcoholism:
    definition of, 20–22, 28
    as disease, 20–22, 24–28
    myths about, 15–18
    origin of word, 23
    path to, 44–62
    statistics on, 18–19
American Medical Association (AMA), 20, 22
American Psychiatric Association, 22, 30–31
Antabuse (disulfiram), 89–90
Archer, Loren, 43
Asians, 35
Aversion therapy, 90–91

Bacchus, 115
Begleiter, Henri, 33–34
Bible, 23
Blackouts, 41–42, 55–57, *56*
Blacks, alcoholism among, 35

(124)